Cambridge Elements ≡

Elements in the Philosophy of Immanuel Kant
edited by
Desmond Hogan
Princeton University
Howard Williams
University of Cardiff
Allen Wood
Indiana University

ANTHROPOLOGY FROM A KANTIAN POINT OF VIEW

Robert B. Louden
University of Southern Maine

CAMBRIDGE
UNIVERSITY PRESS

CAMBRIDGE
UNIVERSITY PRESS

University Printing House, Cambridge CB2 8BS, United Kingdom

One Liberty Plaza, 20th Floor, New York, NY 10006, USA

477 Williamstown Road, Port Melbourne, VIC 3207, Australia

314–321, 3rd Floor, Plot 3, Splendor Forum, Jasola District Centre,
New Delhi – 110025, India

79 Anson Road, #06–04/06, Singapore 079906

Cambridge University Press is part of the University of Cambridge.

It furthers the University's mission by disseminating knowledge in the pursuit of
education, learning, and research at the highest international levels of excellence.

www.cambridge.org
Information on this title: www.cambridge.org/9781108742283
DOI: 10.1017/9781108592871

First published 2021

A catalogue record for this publication is available from the British Library.

ISBN 978-1-108-74228-3 Paperback
ISSN 2397-9461 (online)
ISSN 2514-3824 (print)

Anthropology from a Kantian Point of View

Elements in the Philosophy of Immanuel Kant

DOI: 10.1017/9781108592871
First published online: February 2021

Robert B. Louden
University of Southern Maine

Author for correspondence: Robert B. Louden, louden@maine.edu

Abstract: Kant's anthropological works represent a very different side of his philosophy, one that stands in sharp contrast to the critical philosophy of the three *Critiques*. For the most part, Kantian anthropology is an empirical, popular, and, above all, pragmatic enterprise. After tracing its origins both within his own writings and within Enlightenment culture, the Element turns to an analysis of the structure and several key themes of Kantian anthropology, followed by a discussion of two longstanding contested features – viz., moral anthropology and transcendental anthropology. The Element concludes with a defense of the value and importance of Kantian anthropology, along with replies to a variety of criticisms that have been leveled at it over the years. Kantian anthropology, the author argues, is "the eye of true philosophy."

Keywords: Kant, anthropology, philosophical anthropology, pragmatic anthropology, moral anthropology, transcendental anthropology

ISBNs: 9781108742283 (PB), 9781108592871 (OC)
ISSNs: 2397-9461 (online), 2514-3824 (print)

Contents

1 Origins

There is no greater or more important investigation for human beings than the cognition of the human being.

Kant, V-Anth/Pillau 25: 733[1]

---

[1] Kant's works are cited by volume and page number in the German *Akademie-Ausgabe* (AA) of his writings, using the abbreviations employed by the journal *Kant-Studien*. When available, I follow (with occasional slight modifications) the translations in *The Cambridge Edition of the Works of Immanuel Kant*. Other translations are my own. The following specific abbreviations are used in this study:

Anth	*Anthropologie in pragmatischer Hinsicht* (AA 7) (*Anthropology from a Pragmatic Point of View*)
BBGSE	*Bemerkungen über die Beobachtungen über das Gefühl des Schönen und Erhabenen* (AA 20) (*Remarks on the Observations on the Feeling of the Beautiful and Sublime*)
BBMR	*Bestimmung des Begriffs einer Menschenracen* (AA 8) (*Determination of the Concept of a Human Race*)
Br	*Briefe* (AA 10–13) (*Correspondence*)
EACG	*Entwurf und Ankundigung eines Collegii der physischen Geographie* (AA 2) (*Plan and Announcement of a Series of Lectures on Physical Geography*)
GMS	*Grundlegung zur Metaphysik der Sitten* (AA 4) (*Groundwork of the Metaphysics of Morals*)
GSE	*Beobachtungen über das Gefühl des Schönen und Erhabenen* (AA 2) (*Observations on the Feeling of the Beautiful and Sublime*)
IaG	*Idee zu einer allgemeinen Geschichte in weltbürgerlicher Absicht* (AA 8) (*Idea for a Universal History with a Cosmopolitan Aim*)
KrV	*Kritik der reinen Vernunft* (cited by the original pagination in the A and B editions) (*Critique of Pure Reason*)
KU	*Kritik der Urteilskraft* (AA 5) (*Critique of the Power of Judgment*)
Log	*Logik* (AA 9) (*The Jäsche Logic*)
MAN	*Metaphysische Anfangsgründe der Naturwissenschaften* (AA 4) (*Metaphysical Foundations of Natural Science*)
MS	*Die Metaphysik der Sitten* (AA 6) (*The Metaphysics of Morals*)
NEV	*Nachricht von der Einrichtung seiner Vorlesungen in dem Winterhalbenjahre von 1765–66* (AA 2) (*Announcement of the Program of His Lectures in the Winter Semester of 1765–66*)
NTH	*Allgemeine Naturgeschichte und Theorie des Himmels* (AA 1) (*Universal Natural History and Theory of the Heavens*)
Päd	*Pädagogik* (AA 9) (*Lectures on Pedagogy*)
PG	*Physische Geographie* (AA 9) (*Physical Geography*)
PhilEnz	*Philosophische Enzklopädie* (AA 29) (*Philosophical Encyclopedia Lectures*)
Prol	*Prolegomena zu einer jeden künftigen Metaphysik* (AA 4) (*Prolegomena to Any Future Metaphysics*)
Refl	*Reflexionen* (AA 14–19) (*Notes and Fragments*)
RezHerder	*Recensionen von J. G. Herders Ideen zur Philosophie der Geschichte der Menshheit* (AA 8) (*Reviews of J. G. Herder's Ideas for the Philosophy of the History of Humanity*)
SF	*Der Streit der Fakultäten* (AA 7) (*The Conflict of the Faculties*)
ÜGTP	*Über den Gebrauch teleologischer Principien in der Philosophie* (AA 8) (*On the Use of Teleological Principles in Philosophy*)
V-Anth/Busolt	*Vorlesungen Wintersemester 1788–89 Busolt* (AA 25) (*Anthropology Busolt*)

In a broad sense, reflection on the nature of human beings has been a key part of philosophy since its birth.[2] Within the Western tradition of thought, for instance, Socrates is a notable paradigm of a thinker for whom philosophical anthropology was central. As Cicero famously remarks in his *Tusculan Disputations*, "Socrates was the first to call philosophy down from the heavens and set her in the cities of men and bring her also into their homes and compel her to ask questions about life and morality and things good and evil" (Cicero 1971, p. 435). Socrates' exclusive focus on questions concerning human nature led Ernst Cassirer to remark that the only universe Socrates knows, "and to which all his enquiries refer, is the universe of man. His philosophy ... is strictly anthropological" (Cassirer 1944, p. 19). And Plato, in his *Theaetetus*, at one point uses Socrates' singular concentration on human nature to characterize philosophy itself: "The question he [viz., the philosopher] asks is 'What is the human being?' What actions and passions properly belong to human nature and distinguish it from all other beings? This is what he wants to know and concerns himself to investigate" (*Theaetetus* 174b, in Plato 1997, p. 193).

Granted, there are counterexamples to this anthropologically oriented style of philosophy. Socrates himself, for instance, was reacting against many of the early ancient Greek philosophers who preceded him, whom he described as students "of all things in the sky and below the earth" (*Apology* 18c, in Plato

V-Anth/Collins	*Vorlesungen Wintersemester 1772–73 Collins* (AA 25) (*Anthropology Collins*)
V-Anth/Fried	*Vorlesungen Wintersemester 1775–76 Friedländer* (AA 25) (*Anthropology Friedländer*)
V-Anth/Mensch	*Vorlesungen Wintersemester 1781–82 Menschenkunde* (AA 25) (*Anthropology Menschenkunde*)
V-Anth/Mron	*Vorlesungen Wintersemester 1784–85 Mrongovius* (AA 25) (*Anthropology Mrongovius*)
V-Anth/Parow	*Vorlesungen Wintersemester 1772–73 Parow* (AA 25) (*Anthropology Parow*)
V-Anth/Pillau	*Vorlesungen Wintersemester 1777–78 Pillau* (AA 25) (*Anthropology Pillau*)
VKK	*Versuch über die Krankheiten des Kopfes* (AA 2) (*Essay on the Maladies of the Head*)
V-Lo/Dohna	*Logik Dohna-Wundlacken* (AA 24) (*The Dohna-Wundlacken Logic*)
V-Met-L2/Pölitz	*Metaphysik L2 Pölitz* (AA 28) (*Metaphysics Pölitz*, Second Set)
V-Met-N/Herder	*Nachträge Metaphysik Herder* (AA 28) (*Metaphysics Herder*)
V-Mo/Collins	*Moralphilosophie Collins* (AA 27) (*Moral Philosophy Collins*)
V-Mo/Mron II	*Moral Mrongovius II* (AA 29) (*Ethics Mrongovius*, Second Set)
V-MS/Vigil	*Die Metaphysik der Sitten Vigilantius* (AA 27) (*The Metaphysics of Morals: Vigilantius's Lecture Notes*)
V-PP/Powalski	*Praktische Philosophie Powalski* (AA 27) (*Practical Philosophy Powalski*)
VvRM	*Von den verschiedenen Racen der Menschen* (AA 2) (*Of the Different Races of Human Beings*)
ZeF	*Zum ewigen Frieden* (AA 8) (*Toward Perpetual Peace*)

[2] Some of the material in this opening section draws on Louden (2021 a, forthcoming a).

1997, p. 19). But the counterexamples have not prevented some authors from venturing "to characterize philosophy itself as a search for 'a definition of man,' and to interpret the great philosophers of the past as each providing a different account of the powers essential to man" (Hampshire 1960, p. 232).[3]

However, during the Enlightenment anthropological reflection came into its own as an autonomous discipline and briefly achieved a higher status than it has enjoyed before or since. Scores of writers became convinced that "the science of man" should either replace philosophy entirely or at least become the main research project of an enlightened era, and they competed against one another in repeated efforts to shape the discipline in accordance with their own personal visions and concerns. A product of the larger effort to emancipate the empirical study of human nature from theologically based inquiries, best captured by Alexander Pope's[4] famous remark, "Know then thyself, presume not God to scan: The proper study of Mankind is Man" (*An Essay on Man*, in Brinton 1956, p. 57), Kant's own work in anthropology is properly situated within this larger anthropological turn of the Enlightenment.

Kant's best-known anthropological work is *Anthropology from a Pragmatic Point of View* (1798), a late text that he describes as "the present manual for my anthropology course" (Anth 7: 122 n.). He began offering an annual lecture course on anthropology in the winter semester of 1772–3, a practice he con-tinued up until his retirement from teaching in 1796, but his anthropology lectures (numerous transcriptions of which have also been published over the years) themselves draw on – and are in part outgrowths of – still earlier work, particularly his lectures on metaphysics and physical geography. Volume 15 of the Academy Edition of Kant's writings also contains nearly 1,000 pages of additional material relevant to his anthropology lectures – viz., "*Reflexionen zur Anthropologie*" (Notes on Anthropology) and "*Collegentwürfe*" (drafts of the anthropology lectures from the 1770s and 1780s).

Kant began lecturing on metaphysics in the winter semester of 1755–6 when he was an unsalaried *Privatdozent*, and over the years his main text for this course was the fourth edition (1757) of Alexander Baumgarten's *Metaphysica* (see Baumgarten 2013). The part of Baumgarten's long text that is most relevant to the development of Kant's anthropology is the "Empirical Psychology" chapter (§§ 504–739) in "Part III: Psychology" (§§ 501–799), for he also used this same material on empirical psychology as his text when he later began lecturing on anthropology in 1772. Essentially, the first part of Kant's mature

---

[3] For further discussion of the history of philosophical anthropology, see Louden (forthcoming b).

[4] Pope was Kant's favorite poet. For instance, in his early work, *Universal Natural History and Theory of the Heavens* (1755), he cites Pope's *Essay* (from Barthold Heinrich Brocke's German translation) six times (see NTH 1: 241, 259, 318, 349, 360, 365).

anthropology – the "Didactic" – follows Baumgarten most closely, while the second part – the "Characteristic" – stems more from his lectures on physical geography. Although Baumgarten only explicitly uses the term "anthropology" in one passage in his *Metaphysics*,[5] many of the specific topics that Kant discusses in the first part of his anthropology lectures (the cognitive faculty, the senses, pleasure and displeasure, memory, imagination, and so forth) reveal Baumgarten's influence. (However, what Kant says about these topics often diverges from Baumgarten.) And we know that students in the earlier versions of Kant's metaphysics course did at least hear something about the anthropological dimension of Baumgarten's text. Herder, for instance, in his notes from the 1762 course, writes: "Metaphysics contains (1) anthropology" (V-Met-N/ Herder 28: 911).

Kant develops his anthropology partly out of Baumgarten's empirical psychology largely because – unlike Baumgarten – he believes that empirical psychology is not properly part of metaphysics[6] and needs a new home. Metaphysics correctly conceived "has solely *Conceptus puri* [pure concepts] or concepts which are either given through reason or yet at least whose ground of cognition lies in reason as its theme" (V-Anth/Parow 25: 243), and therefore "empirical psychology belongs to metaphysics just as little as empirical physics does" (V-Anth/Collins 25: 7–8). As he writes toward the end of the *Critique of Pure Reason*:

> Empirical psychology must therefore be entirely banned from metaphysics
> .... It is ... merely a long-accepted foreigner, to whom one grants refuge for a
> while until it can establish its own domicile in a complete anthropology (the
> pendant to the empirical doctrine of nature). (KrV A 848–9/B 876–7; cf.
> Mensch 2018, p. 201)

The geographical roots of Kant's anthropology are a bit different, in part because he did not use a text for his course on physical geography.[7] He began

---

[5] "Therefore, philosophical and mathematical knowledge of the human being is possible (§ 249), i.e. philosophical ANTHROPOLOGY and mathematical ANTHROPOMETRY, just as is empirical anthropology through experience" (Baumgarten 2013, § 747). For discussion of Baumgarten's influence on Kant's anthropology, see Lorini (2018).

[6] In his *Metaphysical Foundations of Natural Sciences* (1786), Kant also argues that empirical psychology (along with chemistry, biology, and a host of other disciplines) is not a genuine science because "there can only be as much *proper* science as there is *mathematics* therein" (MAN 4: 470). As a result, "the empirical doctrine of the soul must remain even further from the rank of a properly so-called science than chemistry" (MAN 4: 471). For discussion of the scientific status of Kantian anthropology, see Louden (2014 c).

[7] Minister of Education Karl Abraham von Zedlitz specifically exempted Kant's geography course from the required textbook regulation of the time on the ground that "it is known that no entirely suitable textbook is yet available" (Vorländer 2003, 2: 57). For more detailed discussions of the relationship between Kant's geography and anthropology lectures, see Louden (2011, pp. 121–35; 2014 a).

lecturing on physical geography in the summer semester of 1756, and from the start the study of human beings loomed large in the course. For instance, in his 1757 Announcement for the class, Kant explains that one of its main goals is "to explain the inclinations of human beings that spring from the zone in which they live, the diversity of their prejudices and way of thinking, insofar as this can serve to acquaint man better with himself" (EACG 2: 9). Similarly, in his 1765 Announcement, he notes that the second part of the course "considers the *human being*, throughout the world, from the point of view of the variety of his natural properties and the differences in that feature of man which is moral in character" (NEV 2: 302).

In Kant's view, physical geography and anthropology form two parts of a larger whole. The overriding goal of each course was to provide students with *Weltkenntnis* – literally, "knowledge of the world," but in Kant's sense a practic- ally oriented kind of know-how intended to help students find their way and feel at home in the world at large after they leave the cloistered life of academia. Already latent in this stress on *Weltkenntnis* is what will eventually become Kant's primary marker for his own distinctive approach to anthropology; viz., "pragmatic." As he writes in an essay on race first published in 1775 that also served as an Announcement for the geography course: "*Weltkenntnis* serves to procure the *pragmatic* element for all otherwise acquired sciences and skills, by means of which they become useful not merely for the *school* but rather for *life* and through which the accomplished apprentice is introduced to the stage of his destiny, namely, the *world*" (VvRM 2: 443; cf. V-Anth/Collins 25: 9, V-Anth/ Fried 25: 469, V-Anth/Pillau 25: 733, V-Anth/Mron 25: 1210, Anth 7: 120). Essentially, the study of physical geography helped students acquire *Weltkenntnis* regarding the external world of nature, while the study of anthropology enabled them to learn more about human nature. As Kant notes in the preface to Friedrich Theodor Rink's edited version of the *Physical Geography* lectures: "The experi- ences of *nature* and the *human being* together constitute *knowledge of the world*. *Anthropology* teaches us *knowledge of the human being*, we owe our *knowledge of nature* to *physical geography*" (PG 9: 157).

For well over a century, German scholars have tried to locate the origins of Kant's anthropology lectures exclusively in either his lectures on metaphysics or his lectures on physical geography, with neither side achieving a decisive victory.[8] And this is not surprising, for the reductionist either-or strategy of the participants in the debate fails to do justice to the richness and diversity of Kantian anthropology. A third obvious source is Kant's discussion of the differences of character between the sexes, races, and nations in the third and

---

[8] For an overview and assessment of the debate, see Wilson (2006, pp. 15–26; 2018).

fourth sections of his popular 1764 work, *Observations on the Feeling of the Beautiful and Sublime* – topics that feature prominently in the second part ("Characteristic") of the anthropology lectures.[9] And the concluding section on education in the *Friedländer* anthropology lecture (1775–6), particularly its strong praise of Johann Bernhard Basedow's experimental school, the Philanthropinum ("the greatest phenomenon which has appeared in this century for the improvement of the perfection of humanity" [V-Anth/Fried 25: 722–3; cf. V-Mo/Collins 25: 471]), reveals a further connection to Kant's work in the philosophy of education; viz., his *Lectures on Pedagogy* (first published in 1803 but stemming from lectures first presented in 1776–7) and his two short *Essays Regarding the Philanthropinum* (1776–7). Finally (though here the causal connection proceeds from the anthropology outward), the strong teleological assumption concerning the destiny or vocation (*Bestimmung*) of the human species that is a major motif throughout the anthropology lectures also links them to Kant's later publications in the philosophy of history. As others have argued, Kant's "philosophy of history is a component of the anthropology" (Brandt and Stark 1997, p. liii), for "the origin of most of Kant's assumptions concerning the historical development of humanity … lies in his anthropology lectures" (Sturm 2009, p. 355).

In sum, "Kantian anthropology is an eclectic venture – one that reveals different origins, competing concerns and aims, and multiple application possibilities" (Louden 2000, p. 64). And if one is concerned with the ideas and arguments within Kantian anthropology, it is best to consider them in conjunction with Kant's related work in education, history, politics, religion, and still more "fields of impurity" (Louden 2000, p. 26), each one of which makes a key contribution to his extensive efforts to develop an empirically based theory of human nature.

2 Structure and Key Features

2.1 Structure

Kant usually divided his anthropology into two parts, and, as noted earlier, the influence of Baumgarten's empirical psychology is most noticeable in the first part, where Kant discusses topics such as human cognitive powers, the feeling of pleasure and displeasure, and the faculty of desire (cf. Baumgarten 2013, § 519 ff., § 655 ff., § 663 ff.).[10] The second part, particularly in its discussions of the character of the sexes, peoples, races, and species, reveals more the influence of Kant's 1764 *Observations* and his lectures on physical geography.

---

[9] For more on the relationship between Kant's anthropology and the *Observations*, see Louden (2011, pp. 150–63).

[10] This section borrows a bit from Louden (2000, pp. 70–1, 48–9).

However, over the years Kant labeled the two parts somewhat differently, and he was often rather loose with his terminology. In the 1798 *Anthropology*, Part I is called "Anthropological Didactic" (Anth 7: 123); Part II, "Anthropological Characteristic" (Anth 7: 124). In *Busolt* (1788–9, the shortest of the seven anthropology transcriptions published in volume 25 of the Academy edition), these terms are not used as subdivisions of anthropology, though in the prolegomena we read that "anthropology is properly a *characteristic*" (V-Anth/Busolt 25: 1437) and the final chapter is entitled "Of the Characteristic of the Person" (25: 1433). The Table of Contents for *Mrongovius* (1784–5) includes a "Second, or Practical, Part of Anthropology, which Concerns the Characteristic of the Human Being" (V-Anth/Mron 25: 1208), but no name for the first part. However, at the beginning of the second part the transcriber writes: "As the first part of anthropology contains the physiology of the human being and thus, as it were, the elements out of which the human being is composed, so the practical part of anthropology is the one that teaches us how human beings are constituted in their voluntary actions" (V-Anth/Mron 25: 1367). Similarly, the Contents for *Menschenkunde* (1781–2, first published in 1831) concludes with a "Characteristic" (though it is not labeled "Part II"), the first chapter of which is entitled "Of the Characteristic of the Human Being" (V-Anth/Mensch 25: 852), but the term "Didactic" does not appear. In the Contents for *Pillau* (1777–8) neither of the two terms appears, but Kant uses the term "Characteristic" for the first time later in this lecture transcription when he states: "The Characteristic. It serves to distinguish the characters [*Charactère*]. Character means nothing other than a general mark to distinguish people" (V-Anth/Pillau 25: 814). In the Contents for *Friedländer* (1775–6) there is a "Part II: Anthropology" (V-Anth/Fried 25: 468), but no Part I. However, at the beginning of Part II the transcriber writes: "After we have, in the general part, come to know the human being according to his powers of soul and his faculties, we must now, in the particular part, thus seek to apply the knowledge of the human being, and to make use of it" (V-Anth/Fried 25: 624). In the Contents for both *Parow* and *Collins* (1772–3), the lectures are not divided into two parts, and neither the term "Didactic" nor "Characteristic" appears.

So Kant settled on the terms "Didactic" and "Characteristic" as a way of describing the two parts of his anthropology rather late. But what does he mean by these terms? In the margins of the *Handschrift* (his handwritten manuscript) for the 1798 *Anthropology*, there is a note at the beginning of Part II that reads:

Anthropology 1st Part Anthropological *Didactic* What is the human being?
2nd Part Anthropological *Characteristic* How is the peculiarity of each human being to be cognized?

The former is as it were the doctrine of elements of anthropology, the latter is the doctrine of method. (Anth 7: 410)

This note indicates that Kant is employing the same "Doctrine of Elements/ Doctrine of Method" division that he also uses in his three *Critiques*, the second half of the *Metaphysics of Morals*, as well as several of the lectures on logic (see, e.g., Log 9: 89, 137; V-Lo/Dohna 24: 701, 779). And in the *Dohna* transcription of Kant's anthropology lecture (1791–2 – only a few passages from this transcription are included in volume 25 of the Academy edition), anthropology is explicitly divided into two parts – "The Doctrine of Elements" (Kowalewski 1924, p. 69) and "The Doctrine of Method or Characteristic" (Kowalewski 1924, p. 70; cf. 289–90). In *Busolt*, the penultimate chapter is also entitled "Doctrine of Method" (V-Anth/Busolt 25: 1433).

In the *Critique of Pure Reason*, Kant explains that a doctrine of elements is concerned with estimating and determining the "building materials" of thought and with figuring out "what sort of edifice, with what height and strength" (KrV A 707/B 735) these materials are best suited for. A doctrine of method, on the other hand, is more concerned with the practical application of the materials – how to make them effective in real life. More generally, Kant's doctrine of elements/doctrine of method distinction is a "theory/practice" contrast, and it "might indeed provide a better indication of the structure of the *Anthropology* than the published headings" (Schmidt 2007, p. 169).[11]

2.2 Key Features

2.2.1 Pragmatic

In *Anthropology from a Pragmatic Point of View* and elsewhere, Kant uses the adjective "pragmatic" to describe his own approach to anthropology, and while other German Enlightenment authors such as Wolff, Mendelssohn, and Herder all used this term earlier (for references, see Brandt and Stark

---

[11] Brandt and others draw skeptical conclusions regarding Kant's different ways of dividing up anthropology: "Kant is not successful in finding a satisfactory conceptual solution for the relation of the two parts of anthropology" (Brandt 1994, p. 26; cf. Brandt and Stark 1997, p. xxx; Hinske 1966, p. 426). I concur that Kant's organization of the lectures is sometimes a bit of a "hodgepodge" (Zammito 2014, p. 238), but I do think the theory/practice division described earlier that Kant employs in many of his best-known works is also used to structure the anthropology, and that this provides a clearer sense of what he is up to. However, it is important to remember that even in the opening "theoretical" part, the topics are treated pragmatically. For example, the discussion of memory in the Didactic is intended "to stimulate memory in order to enlarge it or make it agile" (Anth 7: 119). And in the discussion of mental illness, Kant's main goal is to strengthen "human theoretical and practical faculties through knowledge about the sources of their own flaws" (Sánchez Madrid 2018, p. 147).

1997, 25: pp. xiv–xv), "pragmatic" is by far the most famous marker for Kantian anthropology.[12] But what does Kant mean by it?

One thing he is trying to do is differentiate his anthropology from the physiological anthropology championed by Ernst Platner and other philosopher-physicians such as Julien Offray de la Mettrie. In 1772 – the same year that Kant began lecturing on anthropology – Platner published *Anthropology for Physicians and Philosophers*, and Kant's former student Marcus Herz (himself a physician) reviewed the book. Kant, in an often-cited 1773 letter to Herz, emphasizes that his own approach to anthropology is "quite different" (Br 10: 145) from Platner's, and he criticizes Platner's "futile inquiries into the manner in which bodily organs are connected to thought" (Br 10: 146). Although Kant himself was a frequent contributor to medical approaches to the study of human nature,[13] even commenting at one point, "I see nothing better for me than to imitate than the method of the physicians" (VKK 2: 260), he was firmly convinced that their perspective was too reductionist, since it did not take proper account of human freedom. In the preface to his *Anthropology*, he describes the differences between the two approaches as follows: anthropology "can exist either in a *physiological* or in a *pragmatic* point of view. – Physiological knowledge of the human being concerns the investigation of what *nature* makes of the human being; pragmatic, what *he* as a free-acting being makes of himself, or can and should make of himself" (Anth 7: 119).

In the preamble to *Friedländer*, Platner's approach to anthropology is also criticized for being overly speculative and bearing "no relation to the prudent conduct [*klugen Verhalten*] of human beings" (V-Anth/Fried 25: 472). In Kant's own approach, by contrast,

> human beings are not studied in speculative terms, but pragmatic, in the application of their knowledge according to rules of prudence [*Klugheit*], and this is anthropology .... [W]e must therefore study humanity, not however psychologically or speculatively, but pragmatically. For all pragmatic doctrines are doctrines of prudence [*Klugheits Lehren*], where for all our skills we also have the proper means to make proper use of everything. (V-Anth/Fried 25: 470–1; cf. V-Anth/Mron 25: 1211)

This prudential dimension of pragmatic anthropology emphasizes the acquisition of skill in choosing appropriate means toward human happiness, a skill that

---

[12] For related discussion, see Louden (2011b, pp. 67–70, 81–3).

[13] See *Essay on the Maladies of the Head* (1764), *Review of Moscati's Work: On the Essential Corporeal Differences Between the Structure of Animals and Human Beings* (1771), *Note to Physicians* (1782), the third essay in *Conflict of the Faculties* (1796 – "The Conflict of the Philosophy Faculty with the Faculty of Medicine"), and *From Soemmerring's "On the Organ of the Soul"* (1796).

presupposes knowledge of human nature. As he remarks in *Parow*: "The capacity to choose the best means to happiness is prudence" (V-Anth/Parow 25: 413; cf. GMS 4: 416, KrV A 800/B 828).[14]

A second sense of prudence emphasized in Kant's lectures on anthropology concerns reasoning not in the employment of happiness but rather in using other people to achieve one's ends, whatever these ends may be. In *Mrongovius* he states: "prudence is a proficiency or knowledge in reaching one's aims, and making use of this skill or using other human beings for one's aims" (V-Anth/ Mron 25: 1210). And in *Menschenkunde*: "Prudence is ... based merely on knowledge of the human being, by virtue of which we are in a position to direct others according to our purpose" (V-Anth/Mensch 25: 855; cf. Anth 7: 322). This "skill in using others" sense of prudence is also a key part of Kantian anthropology: "Anthropology teaches us ... how we can use human beings to our end. The rules of prudence are taught not in the schools but in knowledge of the world" (V-Anth/Busolt 25: 1436).

But doesn't learning how to rationally manipulate other people violate one of the most famous tenets of Kantian ethics; viz., never to treat human beings merely as means (see GMS 4: 429)? Kant probably meant that anthropology teaches us how to skillfully use other people to achieve our aims *under moral constraints*, but he does not explicitly say this. And in principle, nothing seems to prevent successful students of Kantian anthropology from using their newly acquired prudence for immoral ends.

2.2.2 Empirical (Mostly)

In virtually all of Kant's descriptions of his anthropology, he stresses its empirical nature.[15] For instance, in his 1773 letter to Herz in which he discusses the new course with his former student, he describes it as a *"Beobachtungslehre* [observation-based doctrine]" (Br 10: 146). In the opening sentence of the *Collins* transcription, he states that anthropology is a "science" in which "the grounds of cognition are taken from observation and experience [*Beobachtung und Erfahrung*]" (V-Anth/Collins 25: 7). In the opening section of the *Parow* transcription, where anthropology's connection to empirical psychology is stressed, Kant states that anthropology "deserves a special set of lectures, in part because it does not at all belong to metaphysics" (V-Anth/Parow 25: 244). In the preamble to *Friedländer*, he asks: "How does anthropology arise? Through the collection of many observations [*Beobachtungen*] about human beings by those authors who

---

[14] For further discussion of the place of prudence in Kant's anthropology, see Wilson (2018, pp. 15–26) and Kain (2003).

[15] This section borrows a bit from Louden (2018 a).

had acute knowledge of human beings" (V-Anth/Fried 25: 472). In the *Menschenkunde* transcription, Kant announces that his purpose is "merely to draw up rules from the multiplicity that we perceive [*wahrnehmen*] in human beings" (V-Anth/Mensch 25: 856). In the introduction to *Mrongovius* (1784–5), he emphasizes that we acquire knowledge of the human being "more from experiences than precepts [*mehr aus Erfahrungen als Vorschriften*]" (V-Anth/ Mron 25: 1210). And in the prolegomena to *Busolt* (1788–9), Kant states: "when this observation [*Beobachtung*] of human beings (*anthropography*) is brought to a science, it is called 'anthropology'" (V-Anth/Busolt 25: 1435). Finally, in the preface to his own text, *Anthropology from a Pragmatic Point of View*, in his brief discussion of some of the important "aids [*Hilfsmittel*]" to anthropology – "world history, biographies, even plays and novels" (Anth 7: 121) – Kant again stresses the empirical nature of his anthropology when he remarks that even in the case of the overdrawn characters of "a Richardson or a Molière, the *main features* must have been taken from the *Beobachtung* of the real actions of human beings: for while they are exaggerated in degree, they must nevertheless correspond to human nature in kind" (Anth 7: 121).

And in still other texts where Kant refers to a crucial but contested subfield of his anthropology – viz., *moral* anthropology (discussed in more detail later) – the empirical character of the discipline is again emphasized. For instance, the "*practical anthropology*" mentioned in the preface of the *Groundwork of the Metaphysics of Morals* refers explicitly to "the empirical part [*der empirische Teil*]" of ethics (GMS 4: 388). And the "moral anthropology" discussed briefly in the *Metaphysics of Morals* and elsewhere is "the counterpart of a metaphysics of morals" (viz., the empirical part of morals) that deals only with certain "subjective conditions in human nature" (MS 6: 217). Moral anthropology, he notes in a transcription from one of his ethics courses, is that part of morality "to which the empirical principles [*die empirische Principien*] belong" (V-Mo/ Mron II 29: 599).

In all of these texts, Kant is signaling to readers that his anthropology is fundamentally different from the transcendental philosophy that one finds in his three *Critiques* and for which he is best known. The latter works emphasize a priori knowledge which "has been carefully cleansed of everything empirical" (GMS 4: 388), but Kantian "anthropology rests on empirical data, given through experience" (V-Anth/Busolt 25: 1436). A priori cognition "is opposed to empirical cognition: philosophy concerning this is transcendental philosophy" (Refl 4851, 18: 10), and "[f]rom empirical principles one cannot attain transcendental ones" (Refl 4889, 18: 20). Kant's distinction between empirical and transcendental philosophy is fundamental to his outlook, and while his anthropology is not always as empirical as he claims (similarly, the *Critiques* may not always be as pure and nonempirical as he alleges), the fact remains that he believes firmly that his anthropology is a *Beobachtungslehre*.

However, one important qualification concerning the alleged empirical status of Kantian anthropology involves a distinction between what Kant calls "local" and "general" anthropology. In *Friedländer*, he emphasizes that his

> [a]nthropology is not however a local [*locale*], but a general [*generale*] anthropology. In it one comes to know the nature of humanity, not the state of human beings, for the particular properties of human beings always change, but the nature of humanity does not. Anthropology is thus a pragmatic knowledge of what results from our nature, but it is not a physical or geographical knowledge,[16] for that is tied to time and place, and is not constant .... [A]nthropology is not a description of human beings, but of human nature. (V-Anth/Fried 25: 471)

A similar distinction occurs in *Pillau*, where Kant contrasts the general *Weltkenntnis* that a man of the world possesses with the merely local *Weltkenntnis* possessed by merchants. When knowledge of the human being "is treated pragmatically, then it is *Weltkenntnis* and forms a man of the world [*bildet einen Weltmann*]" (V-Anth/Pillau 25: 733). And this pragmatic, general *Weltkenntnis* that the *Weltmann* has acquired is then distinguished from the merely "local *Weltkenntnis* which merchants [*Kaufleute*] have" (V-Anth/Pillau 25: 734).[17]

Kantian anthropologists are thus charged with finding core truths about human nature, and this quest for universal truths about the human condition does set them at odds with "the relativist bent" (Geertz 2000, p. 44) that is

---

[16] In the 1798 *Anthropology*, Kant uses this distinction between pragmatic and physical or geographical knowledge to exclude discussions of race from pragmatic anthropology. In the preface, he writes: "even knowledge of the races of human beings as products belonging to the play of nature is not yet counted as pragmatic knowledge of the world, but only as theoretical knowledge of the world" (Anth 7: 120). However, several of the earlier transcriptions of his annual anthropology course contain a section devoted to the discussion of race. See, for example, V-Anth/Mensch 25: 1187–8 and V-Anth/Parow 25: 840–3. For further discussion, see Section 4.

[17] The transcriber of *Pillau* goes on to state that this general *Weltkenntnis* "is not empirical [*nicht empirisch*] but cosmological" (V-Anth/Pillau 25: 734) – a claim that would appear to contradict Kant's frequent assertions that his anthropology is an empirical science. I think *Pillau* is in error here. Cosmological knowledge (at least in the context of Kant's anthropology) *is* empirical knowledge, but it is broad-based empirical knowledge that places a priority on the whole rather than the parts. As Kant writes in the 1775 Announcement of his lecture activity, both physical geography and anthropology "must be considered *cosmologically*, namely, not with respect to the noteworthy details that their objects contain (physics and empirical psychology) but with respect to what we can note of the relation as a whole in which they stand and in which everyone takes his place" (VvRM 2: 443; cf. PG 9: 157). Similarly, in yet another anthropology transcription, he states: "In order to have knowledge of the world, one must study a whole, out of which the whole parts can hence be determined, and that is a system, so far as the manifold originates from the idea of the whole" ("*Ms. 400*," as cited by Brandt and Stark 1997, p. xxxix).

implicit in much subsequent cultural anthropology. Kantian anthropologists do subscribe to "a context-independent concept of 'Human Nature'" (Geertz 2000, p. 50). As Kant remarks in his 1765 *Announcement* when he emphasizes the centrality of "the study of *man*" in his ethics lectures: "And by *man* here … I mean the *nature* of man, which always remains [*die immer bleibt*], and his distinctive position within the creation" (NEV 2: 311).

2.2.3 Cosmopolitan

In the preface to his 1798 *Anthropology*, Kant adds a further qualification to the kind of general *Weltkenntnis* his anthropology seeks. Anthropology is only properly called "pragmatic," he stresses, "when it contains knowledge of the human being as a *citizen of the world* [*als Weltbürgers*]" (Anth 7: 120). Now a normative dimension is added to the quest for a general account of human nature, albeit one that is still arrived at empirically. Pragmatic anthropology's investigation of human nature will, Kant holds, uncover the cosmopolitan character of our species. In the final section of the *Anthropology* where he discusses the character and vocation of the human species, Kant returns to the issue of our cosmopolitanism character when he writes: "The character of the species, as it is known from the experience of all ages [*aus der Erfahrung aller Zeiten*] and by all peoples, is this: that … they feel destined by nature [*von der Natur bestimmt*] to [develop] … into a *cosmopolitan society* [*weltbürgerliche Gesellschaft*] (*cosmopolitanismus*)" (Anth 7: 331; cf. V-Anth/Fried 25: 696).[18] Kant's strong teleological commitment in his anthropological works – his acceptance of the "principle that nature wants every creature to reach its destiny [*Bestimmung*] through the appropriate development of all predispositions [*alle Anlagen*] of its nature" (Anth 7: 329) – enables him to inject a prescriptive dimension into his account of human nature. In pointing to natural developmental structures within the human species, he is able simultaneously to describe what presently is the case as well as what, in the future, ought to be the case. But the normative dimension implied in humanity's *Bestimmung* is one that comes out of nature itself (or so Kant claims).[19]

2.2.4 Popularity

Yet another core dimension of Kantian anthropology is its popular, anti-scholastic orientation. In *Menschenkunde*, Kant criticizes Platner for having merely

---

[18] For related discussion, see Louden (2014 b).

[19] At the same time, the strong teleological dimension of Kantian anthropology may put undue strain on its claim to be a *Beobachtungslehre*. As Kant remarks in the third *Critique*, the concept of purposiveness "is a special a priori concept that has its origin solely in the reflecting power of judgment" (KU 5: 181).

"written a scholastic anthropology" (V-Anth/Mensch 25: 856), and in *Mrongovius* the empirical psychology chapter in Baumgarten's *Metaphysics* is similarly chided: "his book only concerns what is scholastic" (V-Anth/Mron 25: 1214). The scholastics produced "science for the school, but one could not obtain any enlightenment for common life from it" (V-Anth/Mensch 25: 853). Their "brooding sciences ... are of no utility to the human being" (V-Anth/ Mensch 25: 853).

By contrast, Kant's anthropology is unabashedly popular in orientation: "Our anthropology can be read by everyone, even by women at the dressing table" (V-Anth/Mensch 25: 856). Similarly, in his 1773 letter to Herz, he boasts to his former student that audience members of his new anthropology course "from beginning to end, find my lectures entertaining and never dry" (Br 10: 146) and that the *Beobachtungslehre* he is trying to develop in the course is "very pleasant [*sehr angenehmen*]" rather than onerous (Br 10: 146; cf. VvRM 2: 429).

Kant's earliest biographers agree with each other in describing the anthropology lectures as the most popular and accessible of all of his courses. Jachmann, for instance, reports that they were

> an extremely pleasant instruction, which were also attended the most frequently. Here one saw the lofty thinker strolling about in the material world, and the human being and nature illuminated with the torch of original reason. His astute remarks ... were fitted out in lectures filled with wit and genius, which charmed every single listener. (Jachmann 1804, p. 31)

And Rink describes the anthropology lectures as "lively," noting that they were enriched by "the keen observations ... [Kant] mixed in, which he drew either from his own experience or from his reading, such as the best English novelists" (Rink 1805, p. 46).

Allen Wood, in commenting on Kant's opposition to scholastic approaches to anthropology, notes:

> Here Kant may be seen as taking up, in his lectures on human nature, the task of a "popular" philosopher, in the tradition of Christian Thomasius and of the Berlin Enlightenment philosophers, such as Garve and Mendelssohn. This was a role that he deliberately declined to play in many areas of philosophy, such as metaphysics, pure moral philosophy, and the new discipline of transcendental philosophy .... But it was one that he apparently thought appropriate for the study of anthropology. (Wood 2012, p. 3)

In sum, Kantian anthropology is pragmatic, prudential, empirical (in the "general" or cosmological sense), cosmopolitan, and popular, and its overriding goal is *Weltkenntnis*. Each of these core dimensions is absent from Kant's better-known writings in metaphysics, epistemology, and pure moral philosophy. But as I shall argue later, when added together they constitute a formidable and important addition to the more familiar Kant. They also point to a different way of doing philosophy, one that is strongly needed at present.

3 Two Contested Issues

3.1 Moral Anthropology

There are two important but contested issues surrounding Kantian anthropology that have each been a source of continual controversy over the years.[20] The first concerns ethics. To what extent do we find a distinctly *moral* anthropology within Kant's anthropology lectures? On the one hand, it cannot be denied that the specific term "moral anthropology" appears nowhere in any of the anthropology lectures. Nor does Kant employ the standard vocabulary of his ethical theory in any of these texts. These linguistic points have led some commentators to conclude that there is no moral anthropology within pragmatic anthropology, and that Kantian anthropology and ethics share nothing in common. Brandt and Stark, for instance, write: "neither in the lecture transcriptions nor in the book version [of the *Anthropology*] are the words 'categorical' or 'imperative' or 'autonomy' cited," from which they conclude that "pragmatic anthropology is not identical in any of its phases of development with the anthropology that Kant repeatedly earmarks as the complementary part [*Komplementärstück*] of his moral theory after 1770" (Brandt and Stark 1997, pp. xlvi–vii, xlvi; cf. MS 6: 217).[21] Or, as Brandt remarks in another essay: "Pragmatic anthropology is ... not the discipline of practical anthropology, variously described by Kant, that was supposed to function as a complement to pure moral philosophy" (Brandt 2003, p. 92). Similarly, Zammito asserts that in Kant's anthropology "the great promise of a 'moral anthropology', included in every one of Kant's writings in ethics, was never fulfilled" (Zammito 2002, p. 301).

3.1.1 Moral Weltkenntnis

Nevertheless, there are multiple considerations that speak against the claim that there is no moral anthropology within Kantian anthropology. The first concerns Kant's frequent remarks about the importance and necessity of acquiring moral *Weltkenntnis*. As we saw earlier, one of the primary goals of Kantian

---

[20] The first part of this section borrows a bit from Louden (2000, pp. 71–4; 2011, pp. 49–104; 2018 b). See also Cohen (2009, pp. 84–108) and Frierson (2003, pp. 48–67).

[21] However, these remarks seem to indicate Brandt's position more than Stark's. Elsewhere Stark writes: "In contrast to Reinhard Brandt, I am of the opinion that an internal, positive relationship exists between Kant's lectures on anthropology and his moral philosophy; more precisely, that the notes of the lectures *indicate* some such relationship" (Stark 2003, p. 21).

anthropology is to provide students with knowledge of the world – more specifically, knowledge of human beings and their place in the world. Granted, this general *Weltkenntnis* can be put to both moral and nonmoral uses, but it is clear that one of the main applications of *Weltkenntnis* that Kant hoped to foster in his anthropology lectures was a distinctively *moral* one. In the prolegomena to *Collins*, for instance, after stating that "knowledge of the world consists in knowledge of the human being," Kant adds: "It is from the lack of it that so many practical sciences, for example moral philosophy, have remained unfruitful .... Most moral philosophers and clergymen lack this knowledge of human nature" (V-Anth/Collins 25: 9). And in several other transcriptions where the multiple "uses [*Nutzen*] of anthropology" are listed, "morals [*Moral*]" is a prominent member of the list (V-Anth/Pillau 25: 734, 735; V-Anth/Mron 25: 1211). Similarly, in Collins' transcription of one of Kant's ethics courses we read:

> Morals cannot subsist [*nicht bestehen*] without anthropology .... People are always preaching about what ought to be done, and nobody thinks about whether it can be done, so that even the admonitions, which are tautological repetitions of rules that everyone knows already, strike us as very tedious, in that nothing is said beyond what is already known, and the pulpit orations on the subject are empty, if the preacher does not simultaneously attend to humanity. (V-Mo/Collins 27: 244)

Moral *Weltkenntnis* is needed in order to make the abstract principles of moral theory efficacious in human life. As Kant remarks in the *Groundwork*, "morals needs anthropology for its *application* to human beings [*Anwendung auf Menschen*]" (GMS 4: 412). On Kant's view (though he also believes that this is common knowledge), true moral norms are nonempirical and apply not just to humans but also to all rational beings throughout the universe. "Everyone must admit [*Jedermann muß eingestehen*] that a law, if it is to hold morally ... does not just hold for human beings, as if other rational beings did not have to heed it; and so with all remaining genuine moral laws [*alle übrige eigentliche Sittengesetze*]" (GMS 4: 389). But in order for humans to effectively apply the a priori norms of Kantian moral theory to their own life situation, they need to acquire moral *Weltkenntnis* – a solid, empirically grounded grasp of human nature and the sociocultural world in which humans live. As Kant remarks in the *Metaphysics of Morals*: "A metaphysics of morals cannot dispense with principles of application, and we shall often take as our object the particular *nature* of the human being [*die besondere Natur des Menschen*], which can only be cognized by experience" (MS 6: 216–17). And providing human beings with these indispensable principles of application to the human condition is the job of moral anthropology: "The counterpart of a metaphysics of morals, the other member of the division of practical philosophy as a whole, would be moral anthropology [*moralische Anthropologie*]" (MS 6: 217; cf. PhilEnz 29: 12).

3.1.2 Hindrances and Helps

A related but more specific point concerns Kant's remark about the task of moral anthropology as described in the *Metaphysics of Morals*. "Moral anthropology," he asserts here, deals "only with the subjective conditions in human nature that hinder people or help them in *carrying out* [*Ausführung*] the laws of a metaphysics of morals" (MS 6: 217). In other words, Kantian anthropologists ask: What is it about *Homo sapiens* that makes acting on moral principle difficult for members of this species (= "hindrances")? As Kant remarks in one of his ethics lectures, "one must see what sorts of hindrances to virtue are to be found in the human being" (V-PP/Powalski 27: 97). Similarly, what can anthropology show us about those specific features of human beings that can aid them in acting morally (= "helps")? In drawing attention to these helps and hindrances, moral anthropology can help a priori moral principles obtain "access" or "entrance [*Eingang*]" (GMS 4: 389) into the human will.

Throughout his writing career, Kant subscribed to the view that although genuine moral principles apply to all varieties of rational beings, different subgroups of these beings (depending on their species-specific biology, physiology, etc.) stand in different relations to these principles. For instance, in his early work, *Universal Natural History and Theory of the Heavens* (1755), he notes that the inhabitants of earth "and perhaps those of Mars" are "in the dangerous middle position, where the temptation of sensible stirrings against the supremacy of spirit has a strong power of seduction," but whose spirit also "cannot deny that it has the capacity to put up resistance" to this temptation (NTH 1: 366). And in the 1798 *Anthropology*, after making the more sober confession that "we have no knowledge [*keine Kenntnis*] of *non-terrestrial* rational beings" (Anth 7: 321; cf. V-Anth Busolt 25: 1437), he nevertheless conjectures that

> on some other planet there might be beings who could not think in any other way but aloud; that is, they could not have any thoughts that they did not at the same time *utter*, whether awake or dreaming, in the company of others or alone. What kind of behavior toward others would this produce, and how would it differ from that of our own human species? (Anth 7: 332)

As part of its general goal of making morality more efficacious in human life, moral anthropology is thus charged with learning more about those specific features of human nature that tend to make morality comparatively difficult or easy for human beings.

Helps. One subjective condition in human nature that helps human beings in adhering to moral principles and which Kant discusses fairly extensively in his *Anthropology* is politeness.[22] Like Rousseau,[23] he is aware of the darker and superficial sides of politeness: "In society everyone is well-behaved, [but] everything is appearance [*alles ist Schein*], the desires of the citizens against each other are there; in acting everyone burns with wickedness" (V-Anth/Mensch 25: 930; cf. V-Anth/Mron 25: 1254, Anth 7: 152). But unlike Rousseau, Kant also sees great value in the practice of politeness among humans, primarily because it can serve as an aid in the development of morality. For politeness "is a step toward virtue" (V-Anth/Mensch 25: 930). Why? Because politeness enables us "to deceive the deceiver within ourselves, the inclinations" (Anth 7: 151). That is, when we practice politeness, we are able to trick our inclinations into following practical reason's demands – for example, to respect the inherent dignity of our fellow human beings. And if this trick is performed successfully, we are on the road to virtue. "In order to save virtue, or at least lead the human being to it, nature has wisely implanted in him the tendency to allow himself willingly to be deceived" (Anth 7: 152; cf. MS 6: 473–4). In human beings, inclinations are often a hindrance to morality, for many of our inclinations stand in conflict with the commands of practical reason. Humans (but not necessarily other rational creatures) are built in such a way that the practice of politeness can serve as an aid in the development of morality. However, if nonhuman moral agents (for instance, Kant's hypothetical "beings who could not think in any way but aloud") tried to engage in acts of politeness, the results would turn out quite differently. There would be many situations where such creatures would not even be able to practice politeness, and in other cases where they did manage to act politely their inclinations would not be sufficiently tricked.

Political institutions – particularly republican regimes, where the rule of law is adhered to and where all citizens play at least an indirect role in legislation by electing representatives – are a second help to morality discussed by Kant. In an important footnote in *Toward Perpetual Peace* (1795), he argues that republican regimes, by instilling nonviolent behavior patterns, disciplining our emotions, and making us less partial toward our own self-interest, help to establish a "moral veneer" over human society, and that in doing so "a great step *toward* morality (though not yet a moral step) is made" (ZeF 8: 375–76 n.). Through

---

[22] For more detailed discussion of this topic, see Louden (forthcoming c).

[23] "Suspicions, fears, coldness, reserve, hate, betrayal will hide constantly under that uniform and false veil of politeness, under that much vaunted urbanity which we owe to the enlightenment of our century" (Rousseau 1964, p. 38).

participation in republican regimes, Kant hopes humans will experience "progress in enlightenment," a progress that will eventually "transform a *pathologically* compelled agreement to form a society finally into a *moral* whole" (IaG 8: 21). Here as elsewhere, the strong influence of Rousseau on Kant's theory of human nature is again noticeable. As he states in *Pillau*: "Rousseau shows how a civil constitution must exist in order for the complete end of human beings to be reached" (V-Anth/Pillau 25: 847).

Hindrances. When it comes to human beings, their affects and passions constitute the main hindrance to morality, for "both affect and passion shut out the sovereignty of reason" (Anth 7: 251). Passion, however, is a stronger hindrance than affect: affect involves "merely a *lack of virtue*," whereas passion is "*properly* evil, that is, a true vice" (MS 6: 408). "Passion is blind" (V-Anth/Mron 25: 1339–40; cf. V-Anth/Fried 25: 592), and "can be conquered only with difficulty or not at all by the subject's reason" (Anth 7: 251), whereas affect refers only "to a feeling of pleasure or displeasure in the subject's present state that does not let him rise to *reflection*" (Anth 7: 251). Affects and passions are thus "essentially different from one another, both with regards to the method of prevention and to that of the cure that the physician of souls would have to apply" (Anth 7: 251). "Affect is distinct from passion. – Affect is like a sudden storm that quickly ceases. But passion is like a continuous gush that does not cease, but grows more and more with time. It can also never be properly extirpated" (V-Anth/Mron 25: 1340; cf. V-Anth/Fried 25: 499). Or, as Kant remarks in his *Anthropology*:

> Affect works like water that breaks through a dam; passion, like a river that digs itself deeper and deeper into its bed. … Affect is like drunkenness that one sleeps off, although a headache follows afterward; but passion is regarded as a sickness that comes from swallowing poison, or a deformity. (Anth 7: 252)

In essence, passions such as hatred and obsessive ambition embed themselves much more deeply in the human soul than affects such as sadness or fear, and the former ultimately cause much more damage than the latter. "Passions are cancerous sores for practical reason, and for the most part they are incurable because the sick person does not want to be cured and flees from the dominion of principles, by which alone a cure could occur" (Anth 7: 266).

In its examination of affects and passions, moral anthropology seeks to explain the differences between them, to show how each hinders morality, and to offer pragmatic advice on how to treat them and hopefully impede their influence. But all of this fits under the broader and more fundamental goal of figuring out what human nature is like in order to more effectively promote moral ends. How, given what we have learned empirically about human nature, can we make morality more efficacious in human life?

Kant's discussions of egoism near the beginning of many versions of the anthropology lectures provide a second example of a major hindrance to morality. Although he refers to several different varieties of egoism (e.g., aesthetic, logical, physical), his remarks on moral egoism are most relevant for our present purposes. "The moral egoist," Kant states in *Busolt*, "is the one who blinds himself so that he places little value on what is outside himself. One must keep a tight rein on this emotion [*Regung*] of self-love" (V-Anth/Busolt 25: 1438; cf. V-Anth/Mensch 25: 859, V-Anth/Mron 25: 1215, 1217). If humans fail to sufficiently constrain their egoism, they will never learn to act on moral principle: "the *moral egoist* limits all ends to himself, sees no use in anything except that which is useful to himself, and as a eudaemonist puts the supreme determining ground of his will simply in utility and his own happiness, not in the thought of duty" (Anth 7: 130).

3.1.3 A Moral Map for Humanity

Yet another key dimension of moral anthropology present in Kant's anthropology lectures, alluded to briefly in our earlier discussion of the cosmopolitan character of Kantian anthropology, is his desire to provide humans with a moral map of their collective destiny – a conceptual orientation indicating where the species is headed, along with programmatic recommendations concerning what needs to be done in order to bring humans closer to their normative destination. Kantian anthropology, as Kaulbach notes, provides human beings with "a plan, a map of the whole, within which one is able to determine one's position and can trace out for oneself the path by which one can reach one's chosen goals" (Kaulbach 1966, p. 61; cf. Cohen 2009, pp. 105–8).

The endpoint indicated on Kant's moral map, as he states in the final sentence of his *Anthropology*, is "a progressive organization of citizens of the earth into and towards the species as a system that is united cosmopolitically [*kosmopolitisch verbunden*]" (Anth 7: 333; cf. V-Anth/Fried 25: 696). In one of his marginal notes to the *Handschrift* of this text, he adds that "there is a cosmopolitical predisposition [*eine cosmopolitische Anlage*] in the human species which, even with all the wars, gradually wins the upper hand in the course of political affairs over the selfish predispositions of people" (Anth 7: 412). But as he also cautions his audience in the *Menschenkunde*, humanity's cosmopolitical unity refers to "a point in time, however, that is still very far away" (V-Anth/Mensch 25: 1202).

The key concept behind the topological and chronological outline of humanity's destiny provided by moral anthropology is the strong teleological assumption that undergirds Kant's anthropology – an assumption that he believes is itself firmly rooted in biology. "In nature everything is designed to achieve its greatest possible perfection" (V-Anth/Fried 25: 694; cf. ÜGTP 8: 179, Päd 9: 445). "Every creature reaches its destiny [*Bestimmung*] in the world; i.e., reaches the time in which all of its natural predispositions [*Naturanlagen*] are developed and come to maturity" (V-Anth/Mron 25: 1417–18; cf. Anth 7: 329). In other words, all biological creatures have inherent purposes or goals that are unique to their species, and nature intends that these goals will eventually be realized. Obviously, however, there is always a luck factor in reaching such goals. An acorn that is deprived of sufficient water and sunlight will not grow into an oak tree. Similarly, humans who are not raised in congenial environments will not see all of their capacities develop. As Kant remarks in *Friedländer*, "a savage Indian or Greenlander ... has the same seeds [*Keime*] as a civilized human being, only they are not yet developed" (V-Anth/Fried 25: 694; cf. V-Anth/Mensch 25: 857).

In the case of humans, however, there are several key features of their *Bestimmung* that distinguish it from the destinies of other organisms. First, humans pursue their *Bestimmung* as free agents who are not irrevocably fated or causally determined to reach it. As a result, humanity's *Bestimmung* is more properly a vocation or calling rather than a destiny, albeit one that is still part of our biological nature. Unlike other creatures, we pursue our *Bestimmung* through acts of free choice and deliberation. Whether or not we humans do eventually progress to a stage where we are cosmopolitically united depends on our own free choices and efforts. It's up to us. As Kant writes in *The Conflict of Faculties* (1798):

> No one can guarantee that now, this very moment, with regard to the physical position of our species, the epoch of its decline would not be liable to occur. ... For we are dealing with free-acting beings, to whom, it is true, what they *ought* to do may be *dictated* in advance, but of whom it may not be *predicted* what they *will* do. (SF 7: 83)

Second, humanity's *Bestimmung* is a collective achievement reached only after many generations of effort and cultural advancement, whereas in the case of all other biological creatures, each individual organism reaches its species' *Bestimmung*. As Kant notes in the *Anthropology*:

> First of all, it must be noted that with all other animals left to themselves, each individual reaches its complete *Bestimmung*; however with human beings only the *species*, at best, reaches it; so that the human race can work its way up to its *Bestimmung* only through *progress* in a series of innumerably many generations. (Anth 7: 324; cf. V-Anth/Mensch 25: 1196, V-Anth/Mron 25: 1417, Refl 1521, 15: 687)

The concept of *"Bestimmung"* has rightly been called "the leading center of Kantian philosophy" (Brandt 2007, p. 7), and in Kantian anthropology it clearly has moral implications. Kantian anthropology "is not just concerned with what human beings are, but what they should make of themselves" (Wilson 2006, p. 36). As Kant himself proclaims in the preface to the 1798 *Anthropology*, pragmatic anthropology investigates what the human being "as a free-acting being makes of himself, or can and should make of himself" (Anth 7: 119). However, as noted earlier, the central role of humanity's *Bestimmung* in Kantian anthropology also threatens to undermine the discipline's empirical status. For if the concept of purposiveness is indeed "a special *a priori* concept" (KU 5: 181), then Kantian anthropology cannot be a mere *Beobachtungslehre*. Similarly, if it is indeed the case that "the *ought*, if one merely has the course of nature before one's eyes, has no meaning whatsoever" (KrV A 547/B 575; see also KU 5: 173), then it is hard to see how the normative implications of humanity's *Bestimmung* can count as genuine moral oughts. For Kant firmly believes that humanity's *Bestimmung* is rooted in our biological nature. It is part of who we are.

3.1.4 Humans-Only Norms

A related way of thinking about the multiple moral messages implicit in Kantian anthropology is to draw attention to the "humans-only" norms that it frequently invokes – norms that, unlike official Kantian moral norms, do not hold "for *all rational beings in general*" (GMS 4: 408; cf. 410 n., 412, 426, 431) but merely for human beings.[24] Humans-only norms thus lack the "necessity and strict universality" (KrV B 4) that Kant associates with a priori cognitions. For they do not apply to all rational agents, but only to some – viz., humans. Humans-only norms, unlike official Kantian moral norms, are impure, a posteriori, and empirical – they are based on general facts (or at least purported general facts) about human nature and the world in which humans live.

Examples of humans-only norms discussed by Kant in the anthropology lectures and related works include the following:

Education. In *Friedländer* Kant states: "No animal requires instruction, but does what it should out of instinct. Human beings, however, who have understanding, must be given instruction" (V-Anth/Fried 25: 724). And in the opening sentence of the *Lectures on Pedagogy*, he asserts this claim even more strongly: "The human being is the only creature that must be educated" (Päd 9: 441). Granted, the claim may be false (perhaps other creatures, terrestrial or

---

[24] Some of the material in this section borrows from Louden (2021 b).

otherwise, also need to be educated). Many of the empirical generalizations made about human beings in Kant's anthropological works (not to mention the works of non-Kantian anthropologists) are based on false data. (For instance, the less said about his remarks on gender and race, the better.) But the fact remains that Kant conceives of education as involving multiple humans-only norms, and some of these norms do bear on morality. For instance, in his description of moral anthropology in the *Metaphysics of Morals*, he states that it "would deal with the development, spreading, and strengthening of moral principles (in education, in schools, and in popular instruction) and with similar other teachings and precepts based on experience" (MS 6: 217). And in the *Anthropology*, human beings' specific need for moral education is stressed repeatedly. The human being needs "to *moralize* himself by means of the arts and sciences" (Anth 7: 324) and "must be *educated* to the good" (Anth 7: 325). The central task of Kantian moral education is the development of character, and the anthropology lectures also contain extensive discussion of this topic. Moral character "is the distinguishing mark of the human being as a rational being endowed with freedom" (Anth 7: 285; cf. V-Anth/Fried 25: 630), and "the acquisition of good character with the human being takes place through education" (V-Anth/Mensch 25: 1172; cf. Päd 9: 481). Accordingly, the anthropology lectures also contain considerable practical advice on how to develop one's moral character, including the following:

a. Not to intentionally say what is false …
b. Not to dissemble …
c. Not to break one's (legitimate) promise …
d. Not to enter into an association of taste with evil-minded human beings …
e. Not to pay attention to gossip derived from the shallow and malicious judgment of others. (Anth 7: 294; cf. V-Anth/Mron 25: 1387–8, 1392)

Beauty. In several of the anthropology lectures Kant situates beauty between agreeableness and the morally good. For instance, in the *Menschenkunde* we read: "The agreeable has some approval, the beautiful greater approval, the good should have universal approval" (V-Anth/Mensch 25: 1108; cf. V-Anth/Mron 25: 1331, V-Anth/Busolt 25: 1513). Kant develops this position in greater detail in the third *Critique*, where he writes: "agreeableness is also valid for nonrational animals; beauty is valid only for human beings [*nur für Menschen*], i.e., animal but also rational beings, the good, however, is valid for every rational being in general" (KU 5: 210). In other words, beauty is a humans-only phenomenon (see V-Anth/Mron 25: 1332), and while other types of rational beings may not share our judgments regarding beautiful and ugly artworks, fundamental moral norms such as the categorical imperative will hold for them as well as for us.

Kant also holds that the experience of beauty helps humans to develop their capacity for moral judgment. "The culture of taste is a preparatory exercise [*Vorübung*] for morality" (Refl 993, 15: 438). For humans, the experience of "the beautiful prepares us to love something, even nature, without interest" (KU 5: 267; see also MS 6: 443), and for humans, beauty even serves as a symbol for morality itself (see KU 5: 351). "Without interest" – that is, for its own sake, rather than as a means to something else. Aesthetic experience teaches humans how to love something freely for its own sake, and this is also a crucial component of moral judgment. Thus, art (for humans, but not for other rational agents) is a means to morality.

Humans-only norms are also implied in Kant's views about politeness and humanity's *Bestimmung*, discussed earlier. In the case of politeness, humans (but not necessarily other types of rational being) ought to practice politeness because politeness promotes moral virtue in human beings. Similarly, human beings ought to work toward cosmopolitical unity, for this is our species' unique vocation. For "a universal *cosmopolitan condition*" is "the womb in which all the original predispositions of the human species will be developed" (IaG 8: 28). Unless and until we reach the goal of cosmopolitical unity, our predispositions will remain underdeveloped.

Obviously, not all norms are moral norms (there are norms in virtually every sphere of life), and this holds for Kant's humans-only norms as well. But the particular examples of humans-only norms just discussed do count as moral norms, and this is true even though they are impure rather than pure, a posteriori rather than a priori, and even though they are only species-specific norms rather than universal trans-species norms. They count as moral norms because they are necessary means to moral ends. And a moral end is "an end that is also a duty" (see MS 6: 382–8) – we are obligated to pursue it. But adopting the necessary means toward an obligatory moral end is also part of our duty, and failure to do so is a sign of irrationality (see GMS 4: 417).

However, these humans-only moral norms are not quite categorical imperatives, for they apply only to human beings rather than to all rational beings. And as we have seen, for Kant all "genuine moral laws" (GMS 4: 389) apply to rational beings throughout the universe. At the same time, however, humans-only norms are not mere hypothetical imperatives. Hypothetical imperatives are desire-based commands ("If you want x, then you must do y"). But in the present case we are dealing with an imperative that has the following structure: "If you are a human being, then you must do y." The antecedent does not describe a subjective desire, and one cannot evade the consequent simply by changing one's desires. Humans-only moral norms are – for humans but not for other rational agents – inescapable duties. And this is true even though they are not genuine categorical imperatives and lack the "strict universality" of transhuman moral norms.

Because humans-only moral norms are empirical norms based on human nature, they constitute the heart of moral anthropology. For here we are talking about "the second part of morals" – "*philosophia moralis applicata*, moral anthropology, to which the empirical principles belong .... Moral anthropology is morality applied to the human being" (V-Mo/Mron II 29: 599). "The first part of morals," on the other hand – viz., "the metaphysics of morals or *metaphysica pura*" – "is built on necessary laws, as a result it cannot be grounded on the particular constitution of a rational being, [such as] the human being" (V-Mo/Mron II 29: 599).

3.1.5 Lexicographic Data

Finally, an additional argument in support of the claim that Kant's pragmatic anthropology does indeed contain a moral anthropology can be gleaned from the remarks of several of Kant's earliest German- and English-language lexicographers and commentators. When these authors discuss Kant's anthropology, they explicitly refer to practical or moral anthropology as constituting one of its main parts.

Mellin, for instance, in the six-page entry on "Anthropologie" in his six-volume *Enzklopädisches Wörterbuch der kritischen Philosophie* (1797–8), begins by noting that Kant's anthropology "divides into two parts, *theoretical* and *practical*" (Mellin 1970, I: 277). "The second part of anthropology," he writes later,

> in the wider sense of the term, is the application of *moral philosophy* [*Moral*] to the characteristic state and situation of the human faculty of desire – to the drives, inclinations, appetites, and passions of the human being, and the hindrances to the carrying out of the moral law, and it deals with virtues and vices. It is the *empirical part* of ethics, which can be called *practical anthropology*, a true *doctrine of virtue*, or *applied philosophy of morals or ethics*. (Mellin 1970, I: 279)

And he continues his discussion of the second part of Kant's anthropology by noting that "the task of practical anthropology is to determine how the *human being* ought to be determined through the moral law; or what the moral laws are to which human beings under the hindrances of feelings, desires, and passions are subject" (Mellin 1970, I: 280).

Similarly, Schmid, in the fourth edition of his *Wörterbuch zum leichtern Gebrauch der kantischen Schriften* (1798; first edition: 1788), also subdivides Kant's anthropology into theoretical and practical parts. Practical anthropology, he writes, is applied and empirical philosophy of morals, a true doctrine of virtue – it is the consideration of the moral law in relation to the human will, whose desires and drives are hindrances to the execution of the moral law. Practical anthropology is supported on the one hand by principles of pure ethics or the metaphysics of morals, and on the other hand by doctrines of theoretical psychology. (Schmid 1976, pp. 62–3)

Finally, Willich, in *Elements of the Critical Philosophy* (1798), based in part on the author's auditing of Kant's courses "between the years 1778 and 1781 … and … again in summer 1792" (Willich 1798, p. iii), also subdivides Kant's anthropology into theoretical and practical branches. "Anthropology," he writes,

signifies in general the experimental doctrine of the nature of man; and is divided by Kant, into 1) *theoretical* or empirical doctrine of mind, which is a branch of Natural Philosophy; 2) *practical*, applied, and empirical Philosophy of Morals; Ethics – the consideration of the moral law in relation to the human will, its inclinations, motives, and to the obstacles in practicing that law. (Willich 1798, p. 140)[25]

These discussions of Kant's anthropology by some of his earliest lexicographers and commentators clearly indicate that his contemporaries did view his anthropology as containing a moral anthropology, and they also track quite well with our earlier descriptions of some of the central features of Kant's moral anthropology, "the other member of the division of practical philosophy as a whole" (MS 6: 217). To be sure, nowhere do we find a fully developed or systematic moral anthropology within Kantian anthropology. But this is hardly to be expected in popular lectures that "can be read by everyone" (V-Anth/Mensch 25: 857). Nevertheless, as I argued earlier, multiple moral messages are clearly present throughout the anthropology writings, and together they provide more than sufficient evidence to support the claim that there is indeed a moral anthropology within Kant's pragmatic anthropology.

3.2 Transcendental Anthropology

A second contested issue surrounding Kantian anthropology concerns transcendental anthropology.[26] To what extent (if any) does Kantian anthropology also contain a transcendental anthropology? Kant's frequent descriptions of his own anthropology as a science that "does not at all belong to metaphysics" (V-Anth/Parow 25: 244; cf. V-Anth/Collins 25: 7–8, V-Anth/Fried 25: 472, Br 10: 146)

---

[25] Linden, in her detailed discussion of the different meanings of the concept of anthropology in the eighteenth century, also notes that "Kant appears to be the one who first made use of the concept of a moral or practical anthropology in the context of the division of his practical philosophy" (Linden 1976, p. 93).

[26] This section builds on Louden (2018 a).

would seem to rule out any connection to a transcendental project that seeks to uncover the a priori requirements for experience, for "from empirical principles one cannot attain transcendental ones" (Refl 4851, 18: 10). But his alluring appeal to the necessity of an "*Anthropologia transcendentalis*" that would provide us with "the self-knowledge of understanding and reason," "without which we have no measure of the dimensions of our knowledge" (Refl 903, 15: 395), has understandably captured the attention of numerous commentators over the years. And while Kant explicitly uses the term "*Anthropologia transcendentalis*" only once in his myriad writings (in Latin, in a posthumously published *Reflexion* or Note), it does link up with another famous text that he repeats several times. In the *Jäsche Logic* we read:

> The field of philosophy in this cosmopolitan sense can be brought down to the following questions:
>
> 1. What can I know?
> 2. What ought I to do?
> 3. What may I hope?
> 4. What is the human being? [*Was ist der Mensch?*]
>
> *Metaphysics* answers the first question, *morals* the second, *religion* the third, and *anthropology* the fourth. Fundamentally, however, one could reckon all of this [*alles dieses*] as anthropology, because the first three questions relate to the last one. (Log 9: 25; cf. V-Met-L2/Pölitz 28: 533–4 and Kant's letter to Stäudlin of May 4, 1793, Br 11: 429)

In describing an anthropology that is able to answer all of philosophy's questions, Kant is clearly referring to something that is not merely empirical, for philosophy is primarily concerned with conceptual questions that data alone cannot answer. And in his conviction that anthropology is the most fundamental and important discipline of all, he is also echoing many earlier Enlightenment authors. Hume, for instance, in the introduction to his *Treatise of Human Nature* (1739–40), writes:

> 'Tis evident, that all of the sciences have a relation, greater or less, to human nature; and that however wide any of them seem to run from it, they still return back by one passage or another. Even *Mathematics, Natural Philosophy, and Natural Religion*, are in some measure dependent on the science of MAN; since they lie under the cognizance of men, and are judged of by their powers and faculties. (Hume 1978, p. xv)

Similarly, Francis Hutcheson, in the preface to his *Inquiry into the Original of Our Ideas of Beauty and Virtue* (1725), declares: "There is no part of philosophy of more importance than a just knowledge of human nature and its various powers and dispositions" (Hutcheson 1994, p. 3).

But where in Kant's anthropology lectures does he explicitly answer or even address the question, "What is the human being?". Where in these lectures does he proclaim that all of philosophy's questions are answered by the information about human nature found therein? The anthropology texts do not pretend to operate on such an extravagantly high level. As we have seen, for the most part they offer readers only a "very pleasant observation-based doctrine" (Br 10: 146). In a lecture first presented in 1938, Martin Buber remarks:

> The most forcible statement of the task set to philosophical anthropology was made by Kant. ... But it is remarkable that Kant's own anthropology, both what he himself published and his copious lectures on man, which only appeared long after his death, absolutely fails to achieve what he demands of a philosophical anthropology. In its express purpose as well as in its entire content it offers something different – an abundance of valuable observations for the knowledge of man, for example, on egoism, on honesty and lies, on fortune-telling, on dreams, on mental disease, on wit, and so on. But the question, what man is, is simply not raised .... It is as if Kant in his actual philosophizing had had qualms about setting the question which he formulated as the fundamental one. ... Certainly Kant in his anthropology has neither answered nor undertaken to answer the question which he put to anthropology – What is man? He lectured on another anthropology than the one he asked for. (Buber 1965, pp. 119–21)

And more recently, Brandt, in his extensive *Kommentar* on Kant's *Anthropologie in pragmatischer Hinsicht*, echoes Buber's observation when he writes: "pragmatic anthropology ... does not answer the question, 'What is the human being?' ... Neither the Lectures on Anthropology nor the *Anthropology* of 1798 refers to the question, 'What is the human being?' as its central problem; they do not mention it once" (Brandt 1999, p. 16).

3.2.1 Transcendental Anthropology Outside of the Anthropology Texts?

While I do think that both Buber and Brandt are a bit harsh in some of their remarks in the last section (Kant clearly does offer readers a wealth of information about and reflection on human nature in his anthropological writings), I do concur that nowhere in these texts does he claim that all of philosophy's questions are answered by anthropology. There is a noticeable gap between Kant's pragmatic anthropology and his more ambitious philosophical claims regarding transcendental anthropology. But this still leaves open the possibility that there exists a transcendental anthropology elsewhere in his writing; viz., in one or more of the three *Critiques*. Many scholars have defended one or another version of this claim over the years. Let us turn to it now.

3.2.1.1 The First *Critique* as Transcendental Anthropology?

This is the most popular option, in part because both Heidegger and Foucault (albeit in very different ways) are associated with it. Heidegger, for instance, in *Kant and the Problem of Metaphysics* (1929), while acknowledging that "the Anthropology worked out by Kant is an empirical one," maintains that "the question as to the essence of metaphysics is the question concerning the unity of the basic faculties of the human 'mind'. The Kantian ground-laying yields [this conclusion]: the grounding of metaphysics is a questioning with regard to the human being, i.e., anthropology" (Heidegger 1997, p. 144). And Foucault, in his *Introduction to Kant's Anthropology* (his complementary doctoral thesis, submitted in 1961), while at one point asserting that "Kant's *Anthropology* ... amounts to nothing more than a collection of empirical examples," and noting that "pure philosophy ... makes no room for anthropology," nevertheless reaches the paradoxical conclusion that "the *Critique* [*of Pure Reason*] ... is buried inside of the text of the *Anthropology*, serving as its framework ... as a structural fact, and it should be envisaged in this way" (Foucault 2008, pp. 108, 73, 74). The structure of Kant's published *Anthropology*, Foucault insists, thus "repeats" (Foucault 2008, p. 92; cf. 88, 103, 104) the structure of the *Critique of Pure Reason*. However, unlike Heidegger, Foucault regards this alleged union of anthropology and philosophy as an intellectual disaster – it has produced nothing but "the anthropological sleep," which in turn has produced "warped and twisted forms of reflection we can answer only with a philosophical laugh," and which "has governed and controlled the path of philosophical thought from Kant until our own day" (Foucault 1973, pp. 340, 343, 342).[27]

A third attempt to locate a transcendental anthropology within the first *Critique* was undertaken by Volker Simmermacher in his 1951 PhD dissertation, *Kants Kritik der reinen Vernunft als Grundlegung einer Anthropologia transcendentalis*. "*Anthropologia transcendentalis*," he writes (alluding to Kant's remark in *Reflexion* 903), "has to develop as a self-knowledge of the understanding of reason, which begins in the *Critique of [Pure] Reason*. There, reason undertakes "the most difficult of all its tasks, namely, that of self-knowledge [KrV A XI]" (Simmermacher 1951, p. 3). More recently, Claudia Schmidt has argued that "Kant does indeed include a transcendental anthropology ... in the *Critique of Pure Reason*" (Schmidt 2007, p. 160; cf. Van de Pitte 1971, pp. 32–48), and Patrick Frierson has described the first *Critique* as containing both a "radically human-centered metaphysics" and a "transcendental anthropology of cognition" (Frierson 2013, p. 14). "Metaphysics and epistemology turn out, in Kant's hands, to be reckoned as (transcendental) anthropology" (Frierson 2013, p. 18).

---

[27] For further discussion of Foucault's interpretation of Kant's anthropology, see Louden (forthcoming d).

A transcendental anthropology within the context of the *Critique of Pure Reason* would need to meet the following two criteria: (1) it would deal with a priori principles of rationality or cognition insofar as (2) they belong specifically and exclusively to human beings (cf. Schmidt 2007, p. 160). That the first *Critique* deals with a priori principles of cognition seems clear enough. For instance, when Kant introduces the term "transcendental" in the introduction, he writes: "I call all cognition *transcendental* that is occupied not so much with objects but rather with our [*unsern*] mode of cognition of these objects insofar as this is to be possible *a priori*. A system of such concepts would be called transcendental philosophy" (KrV A 11–12). But is the second criterion met? Where does Kant claim that the a priori principles of cognition discussed in the *Critique of Pure Reason* hold specifically and exclusively for humans? Granted, he does occasionally seem to talk this way. For instance, in the introduction he also states that a complete system of transcendental philosophy would contain "an exhaustive analysis of all human cognition [*der ganzen menschlichen Erkenntniß*] *a priori*" (KrV A 13/B 27). And he describes "sensibility and understanding" as the "two stems of human cognition [*zwei Stämme der menschlichen Erkenntniß*]" (KrV A 15/B 29). Similarly, later in the Transcendental Aesthetic he describes spatial and temporal intuition as a way of perceiving objects "which is peculiar to us [*die uns eigenthümlich ist*], and which therefore does not necessarily pertain to every being" (KrV A 42/B 59; cf. Schmidt 2007, p. 161).

But these are all metaphorical ways of talking, at best. Transcendental philosophy cannot be concerned exclusively with humans, for humans are contingent, empirical beings, and transcendental philosophy is not concerned with contingent, empirical matters. As Kant writes in a *Reflexion*, where he compares his approach to that of the more empirically oriented Johann Nikolaus Tetens: "*Tetens* investigated the concepts of pure reason merely subjectively (human nature), I investigate them objectively. The former analysis is empirical, the latter transcendental" (Refl 4901, 18: 23). Similarly, in the *Groundwork* he notes: "transcendental philosophy ... sets forth the special actions and rules of *pure* thinking, that is, of thinking by which objects are cognized completely a priori" (GMS 4: 390). But human thinking is impure, not pure. For Kant, the transcendental is broader than the merely human: the transcendental concerns the conditions of possibility for thinking in general (or at least thinking for finite rational beings who are creatures of sensibility and understanding, and who depend upon being affected by the world around them in order to engage in rational activity), not just the conditions for human thinking. Those who seek to reduce the scope of transcendental philosophy to the merely human are guilty of epistemological speciesism. And just as moral status should not be assigned to individuals simply on the basis of their species membership, so epistemological arguments about the necessary conditions for conceiving objects should not be identified with a merely human perspective.

3.2.1.2 Transcendental Anthropology in Kant's Practical Philosophy?

Other authors have sought to locate a transcendental anthropology not in Kant's theoretical philosophy but rather in his practical philosophy. Marcel Niquet, for instance, regards the previously discussed effort to find a transcendental anthropology "in the contours of the critique of theoretical reason" as a move "in the wrong direction," proposing instead that "a Kantian transcendental anthropology has its home in the grounding of practical philosophy, in the critique of practical reason" (Niquet 2001, p. 407). Similarly, Thomas Rentsch, responding to Kant's claim that we need "to work out for once a pure moral philosophy, completely cleansed of everything that might be in some way empirical and belongs to anthropology" (GMS 4: 389), argues that "instead of pushing the merely empirical anthropology completely out of the way and conceiving a supposedly completely anthropology-free 'pure' morals, it would be better to develop a transcendental-critical philosophical anthropology in systematic connection with ethics" (Rentsch 1990, p. 312). Similarly, Schmidt argues that "Kant's 'transcendental anthropology' also includes an account of the *a priori* conditions of practical reason, as these belong to a human subject" (Schmidt 2007, p. 163), and Frierson describes "Kant's moral philosophy as [a] transcendental anthropology of volition," which provides "a priori normative principles for our human powers" (Frierson 2013, pp. 22, 129; cf. Firla 1981, pp. 39–46, Fellini 2008, p. 25).

But most of these efforts[28] to find a transcendental anthropology within Kant's practical philosophy ignore Kant's frequent admonitions that ethics is not merely about humans: "Everyone must admit … that the command: thou shalt not lie, does not just hold for human beings, as if other rational beings did not have to heed it; and so with all remaining actual moral laws" (GMS 4: 389). "Because moral laws are to hold for every rational being as such [*für jedes vernünftige Wesen überhaupt*]" (GMS 4: 412), he holds, "it is of the greatest practical importance not to make" these laws "dependent on the particular nature of human reason" (GMS 4: 411–12). Rather, we must "derive them

---

[28] Frierson is an exception, insofar as he acknowledges that on Kant's view "the pure moral law would apply to other rational beings as well as to human beings" (Frierson 2013, pp. 22–3). But he also claims that "Kant's dismissal of anthropology at the core of morals is really only a dismissal of *empirical* anthropology at that core" (Frierson 2013, p. 23), and this begs the question whether a transcendental anthropology is even possible. As argued earlier, transcendental philosophy cannot merely be a theory of *human* nature, for humans are contingent, empirical creatures, and transcendental philosophy deals with necessary, nonempirical features of cognition.

from the universal concept of a rational being as such" (GMS 4: 412; cf. KrV A 55). Kant's transcendental investigations in his practical philosophy are concerned "not [with] the actions and conditions of human willing in general, which are largely drawn from psychology" (GMS 4: 390), but rather with a priori principles that all rational beings share with one another. As he writes later in the *Groundwork*:

> *Empirical principles* are not fit to be the foundation of moral laws at all. For the universality with which they are to hold for all rational beings regardless of differences – the unconditional necessity that is thereby imposed on them – vanishes if their ground is taken from the *particular arrangement* [*besonderen Einrichtung*] *of human nature*, or the contingent circumstances in which it is placed. (GMS 4: 442)

In both his practical as well as theoretical philosophy, the level of analysis at which Kant's transcendental investigations occur is far above the merely human.

3.2.1.3 Transcendental Anthropology in the Third *Critique*?

Finally, several authors have sought to locate a transcendental anthropology not in Kant's theoretical or practical philosophy but rather in the aesthetics of the third *Critique*. Nobbe, for instance, claims to uncover "a Kantian anthropology on transcendental-philosophical grounding from KU [viz., *Kritik der Urteilskraft*]" (Nobbe 1995, p. 14), Schmidt holds that "Kant does indeed include a transcendental anthropology ... in ... the *Critique of the Power of Judgment*" (Schmidt 2007, p. 160), and Frierson claims that "Kant's *Critique of Judgment* is a transcendental anthropology of the faculty of feeling and the power of judgment that provides that faculty with its regulative principle" (Frierson 2013, p. 42; cf. 32).

At first glance, this particular strategy for finding a transcendental anthropology in Kant's philosophy might seem to have a strong textual warrant. For as noted earlier in our discussion of the human experience of beauty and its role in the development of moral judgment, in the third *Critique* Kant does proclaim that beauty (which he analyzes as an a priori principle of taste) is "valid only for human beings, i.e., animal but also rational beings" (KU 5: 210). And this passage features prominently in the arguments of those who claim to find a transcendental anthropology in the *Critique of the Power of Judgment* (see, e.g., Nobbe 1995, pp. 14–15 and Schmidt 2007, p. 162). Schiller, in his poem *Die Künstler* (1788), also endorses Kant's claim about the exclusively human experience of beauty when he remarks:

> In industriousness, the bees can surpass you.
> In skillfulness, a worm can be your teacher.

Your knowledge you share with privileged spirits.
Art, o human, you alone have. (Schiller 1955, p. 6)

However, Schiller and Kant both seem to be overlooking the possibility that humans might not in fact be the only creatures who are "animal but rational beings"; viz., the only beings who possess both the requisite sensuous and rational nature that would enable them to make judgments of beauty. Kant subscribed to an infinity of possible worlds hypothesis – he believed humans inhabit a universe "in which worlds or systems are only specks of dust in the sunlight compared with the whole of creation" (NTH 1: 352). If one accepts this hypothesis, the odds are high that there are other sensuous and rational beings out there somewhere. And while it is not hard to believe that their views about art might be quite different than ours, it is very hard to believe that the experience of beauty would be completely foreign to them. In one of his metaphysics lectures, Kant himself indicates an openness to the possibility that humans might not be the only creatures who appreciate art: "The general rules of taste hold only for the sensibility of human beings and for beings that have a sensibility the same as theirs" (V-Met/Mron 29: 892).

All of this is admittedly very speculative, but it is also empirical. That is, in order to definitively answer these questions (including the question of whether "beauty is valid only for human beings"), we would need data that we do not currently possess. But this also takes the debate out of the realm of the transcendental and places it back in the empirical. Consequently, the argument that there exists a transcendental anthropology within the third *Critique* also fails.

3.2.1.4 *Transcendental* Anthropology, No; *Philosophical* Anthropology, Yes

I have argued that all of the efforts to find a transcendental anthropology in Kant's philosophy fail. The attempts to locate a transcendental anthropology within his anthropological works fail both because he himself repeatedly insists that his own anthropology "does not at all belong to metaphysics" (V-Anth/Parow 25: 244) and because of the strong scholarly consensus that these works do not in fact contain any sustained transcendental investigations. The attempts to locate a transcendental anthropology outside of the anthropological works (viz., in the three *Critiques*) fail largely because of misunderstandings about the meaning of the term "transcendental" within Kant's philosophy. Transcendental philosophy is concerned with necessary, nonempirical requirements for experience, but humans are contingent, empirical creatures. In Kantian philosophy correctly construed, the transcendental is always sharply distinguished from the empirical and aligned with the a priori.

Nevertheless, I do concur with those who prefer to use the less contentious term "philosophical" in describing Kantian anthropology. (Indeed, it is hard to imagine how an anthropology developed by Kant could be anything but philosophical.) As argued earlier, there are multiple normative and teleological currents in his anthropology that cannot be constrained within the confines of a mere *Beobachtungslehre*. Additionally, the tremendous weight Kant places on the question "What is the human being?" – even if the question remains insufficiently unanswered – indicates a strong conceptual dimension that is absent in mere empirical work. While it is true that Kant himself does not explicitly "describe his anthropology as philosophical" (Brandt and Stark 1997, 25: xii n.), anyone who reads his anthropology carefully cannot help but see its philosophical dimensions.

I also concur with those who believe "that Kant thought the study of man was the ultimate philosophical enterprise" (Weiler 1980, p. 16), and that in placing the question "What is the human being?" at the center of philosophy "he has left a legacy" (Buber 1965, p. 121) for all subsequent philosophical anthropology. However, some skepticism and caution are also in order regarding Kant's claim that an answer to the question "*Was ist der Mensch?*" will itself provide an answer to all of philosophy's questions (see Log 9: 25). For this claim conflicts with Kant's own extraterrestrial commitments. A definitive answer to the question "What is the human being?" is not going to help the "rational creatures that inhabit Jupiter or Saturn" (NTH 1: 359) or any other non-terrestrial place in the universe in their own philosophical investigations. Philosophy is bigger than the merely human, and to claim that all philosophical questions are magically answered if and when someone definitively answers the question "What is the human being?" is grossly reductionist.

Furthermore, even if we remain earthbound and bracket the extraterrestrial hypothesis, I do not think it is true that all of philosophy can be reckoned as anthropology. To assert this is to diminish philosophy's mission. When philosophers ask questions about the existence of God or the nature of reality (or even the nature of morality or aesthetics), they are not necessarily asking questions about human beings or what humans can, should, or may know, do, or hope (cf. Frierson 2013, p. 5). Rather, they may simply be inquiring into the nature of these things – period.

Keeping these provisos in mind and returning to Kant's remarks concerning the question, "*Was ist der* Mensch?", we are then left with the view that *for humans* the question "What is the human being?" is the most important philosophical question. For *Homo sapiens* philosophical anthropology is the most important discipline. And this is true because the human being is "that creature who is constantly in search of himself – a creature who in every moment of his existence must examine and scrutinize the conditions of his existence. In this scrutiny, in this critical attitude toward human life, consists the real value of human life" (Cassirer 1944, pp. 20–1). What remains is then a further articulation and defense of the value and importance of Kantian anthropology in light of the many criticisms and objections that have been leveled at it over the years. I turn next to this task.

4 The Value and Importance of Kant's Anthropology

> If there is any science that the human being needs, it is the one I teach of how to
> fulfill properly that position in creation which is assigned to him and from which he
> is able to learn what one must be in order to be a human being.
>
> Kant, BBGSE 20: 45

Kant's anthropology is important for many reasons, some of which have already been discussed. For instance, our defense of moral anthropology in Section 3 underscores part of the importance of Kantian anthropology: "Without moral anthropology, we are travellers without a map who know neither our destination nor our means of reaching it" (Louden 2011, p. 77). At the same time, however, Kant's anthropology has been the subject of many criticisms over the years. While some of these criticisms are well taken, others are based on misconceptions of what Kantian anthropology seeks to accomplish and/or unwarranted biases against its aims. In this final section my primary goal is to defend Kant's anthropology by responding to some of the most well-known criticisms leveled against it and to vindicate his belief that, for humans, the most important and valuable philosophical task is the study of human nature.

4.1 Starting with Schleiermacher

The status of Kantian anthropology got off to a bad start with the 1799 publication of Friedrich Schleiermacher's devastating and polemical review of *Anthropology from a Pragmatic Point of View*. In the opening sentence of his review, Schleiermacher condemns Kant's text for being "a collection of trivialities" and "a clear portrayal of the strangest confusion" (reprinted in Kant 1980, p. 339). Versions of Schleiermacher's "triviality and confusion" charge have also resurfaced in subsequent discussions of Kant's anthropology, so this is a good place to begin. Here I concur largely with Frierson, who writes:

> Kant's anthropology is particularly prone to this criticism in part because, as
> he proudly announces when he first writes about his course in anthropology,
> he includes "so many observations of ordinary life that listeners [of his
> lectures] have constant occasion to compare their ordinary experience with
> [his] remarks and thus, from beginning to end, find the lectures entertaining

and never dry" (Br 10: 146). This desire to make his lectures popular infects
even Kant's published *Anthropology*, and so one frequently finds tidbits of
anthropological information that hold one's attention but that do not really
deserve the attention they receive. (Frierson 2003, p. 180 n. 23)

As noted in Section 2, one of the cardinal features of Kantian anthropology is
its unabashedly popular orientation. Kant's aim in his anthropology lectures is
not to produce "science for the school" but rather "enlightenment for common
life" (V-Anth/Mensch 25: 853), and this is a type of knowledge that rightfully
belongs "to the whole world" (V-Anth/Mron 25: 1209) rather than to an elite
group of academics. Obviously, those who are intent on "keeping philosophy
pure" (Rorty 1982, p. 19) will necessarily be opposed to Kantian anthropology
precisely because of its popular, anti-scholastic, and empirical credentials. But
"the gnostic ideal" (Rorty 1982, p. 19) of pure philosophy has lost a great deal of
its luster in recent years (in part because more and more contemporary theorists
are "made queasy by the whole idea of the a priori" – see Peacocke 2004, p.
505), and the need for a more popular, empirically sensitive style of philosophy
is once again gaining a hearing. One of the best ways to add legitimacy to this
side of philosophy's mission is to underscore the fact that some of the greatest
philosophers of the past also practiced popular philosophy. The intricacies of
transcendental philosophy are not Kant's only concern. Particularly in his
lecture and teaching activity, he devotes a great deal of energy to the task of
enlightening students about the people and world around them, so that they will
be able to lead (pragmatically and morally) better lives.

In the final sentence of his review, Schleiermacher also denounces Kant's
Anthropology for its "handling of the female sex as an abnormality [*als einer
Abart*]" (Kant 1980, p. 343). This criticism is well taken; indeed, I would extend
it to say that a major weakness of Kant's *Anthropology* is its handling not only of
women but also of all non-Western European men[29] as abnormalities. Kantian
anthropology "is riddled throughout by inaccurate empirical data (i.e., racial,
ethnic, religious, and sexist prejudices)" (Louden 2011, p. 64). A few examples;
first, regarding women:

"Women … are incapable of more serious work [*gröberen Arbeiten*]," and
they "do not have man's perfection in the sciences" (V-Anth/Fried 25: 700,
704). "Of women one must not say that they have a good mind [*ein gutes
Gemüth*]" (V-Anth/Mensch 25: 1158). "Women need no education beyond the

---

[29] And in fact Kant's prejudices are not even confined to women and non-Western European men.
Consider, for instance, his well-known animus against homosexuality: "*sexual union*" "with a
person of the same sex" is "*unnatural*" (MS 6: 277) – it is an activity that "demean[s] the human
being below the beast" (V-MS/Vigil 27: 641; cf. V-Mo/Collins 27: 391). However, Kant does not
pursue this topic directly in his anthropological works.

negative [one], whereby they are kept from crudeness and bad manners" (V-Anth/Fried 25: 705; cf. 706). "As concerns scholarly women, they use their *books* somewhat like their *watch*; that is, they carry one so that it will be seen that they have one; though it is not usually running or set by the sun" (Anth 7: 307; cf. GSE 2: 229–30, Refl 1299, 15: 572, Br 10: 39).

Prominent examples of Kant's views on race in the anthropology lectures include the following:

> There are Four Races on Earth; these are
>
> 1) The American people acquires no culture [*nimmt keine Bildung an*]. It has no incentives .... They hardly speak at all, do not caress one another, also do not care for anything, and are lazy ....
> 2) The Negro race ... acquire[s] culture, but only a culture of slaves; that is, they allow themselves to be trained.
> 3) .... [T]he Hindus have incentives [*Triebfedern*] ... [and] they acquire culture in the highest degree, but only in the arts and not in the sciences. They never raise it up to abstract concepts .... The Hindus always remain as they are, they never bring culture further ....
> 4) The white race contains all incentives and talents in itself .... Whenever any revolutions have occurred, they have always been brought about by the whites, and the Hindus, Americans, and Negroes have never participated in them. (V-Anth/Mensch 25: 1187–8; cf. V-Anth/Pillau 25: 843, Refl 1520, 15: 877–9, PG 9: 316–17, VvRM 2: 432–41, ÜGTP 8: 174 n., 175)
>
> We find nations that do not appear to have progressed in the perfection of human nature, but have come to a standstill, while others, as in Europe, are always progressing. If the Europeans had not discovered America, the Americans would have remained in their condition. And we believe that even now they will attain to no perfection. (V-Anth/Pillau 25: 840; cf. Refl 1499, 15: 781)
>
> If a people in no way improves itself over centuries, then one may assume that there already exists in it a certain natural predisposition which it is not capable of exceeding. The Hindus, the Persians, the Chinese, the Turks, and in general all Oriental peoples belong to this group. (V-Anth/Mensch 25: 1181; cf. Refl 1501, 15: 789)
>
> In Tahiti ... laziness dominates all the inhabitants. (V-Anth/Mron 25: 1422; cf. RezHerder 8: 65, GMS 4: 423)

And finally, a few examples of Kant's views on non-Western Europeans: "The Russian nation ... *is not yet civilized at all, and is less moralized than any other people in the world*" (V-Anth/Mensch 25: 1186; cf. V-Anth/Fried 25: 542, V-Anth/Mron 25: 1369, 1412–13). "The *Spaniard* ... remains centuries behind in the sciences; resists any reform; is proud of not having to work ... [and] is cruel" (Anth 7: 316; cf. V-Anth/Mensch 25: 1183, V-Anth/Mron 25: 1403–4).

"The Italians have many bandits ... and many preparers of poison .... The Italians have the greatest aversion to the court [and] civil police, and the latter are half dishonorable in their eyes" (V-Anth/Mron 25: 1405–6). The Poles "do not respect any law and want to live [in a state] of license" (V-Anth/Fried 25: 674–5). "They [viz., the Poles] are vivacious, but without much wit and inventiveness. We find no good, original authors among them" (V-Anth/Mron 25: 1412; cf. V-Anth/Pillau 25: 835). "Poland ... and Russia ... do not appear to be properly capable of civilization" (V-Anth/Mensch 25: 1185).[30]

In recent years, several commentators have argued that in his later writings Kant "drops his hierarchical account of the races in favour of a more genuinely egalitarian and cosmopolitan view" (Kleingeld 2007, p. 573; cf. 575, 586, 592 – see also Shell 1996, p. 387 n. 23 and Muthu 2003, pp. 183–4). "Kant's second thoughts on race," Pauline Kleingeld (2007) argues, are most evident when we compare his 1798 *Anthropology* to earlier transcriptions from his annual anthropology course. As noted earlier in Section 2, in the preface to the former work Kant declares that discussion of race does not properly belong to pragmatic anthropology – race is a product "belonging to the play of nature" (Anth 7: 120) rather than a result of what human beings as free-acting beings make of themselves, and so it does not count "as pragmatic knowledge of the world, but only as theoretical knowledge of the world" (Anth 7: 120). And in the extremely short section entitled "On the character of the races" toward the end of the *Anthropology*, Kant makes no reference to the alleged hierarchy of the races and opens with the following remark: "With regard to this subject [viz., race] I can refer to what Herr Privy Councilor *Girtanner*[31] has presented so beautifully and thoroughly in explanation and further development in his work (in accordance with my principles)" (Anth 7: 320). In other words, the 1798 *Anthropology*, even though it contains a section entitled "On the character of the races," contains very, very little discussion of race, and no explicit assertions concerning the alleged hierarchy of the human races.

However, much as I would like to believe otherwise, I remain doubtful that Kant in his later years finally abandoned his hierarchical account of the human races to replace it with "a more generally egalitarian and cosmopolitan view." My doubts are based primarily on the following two reasons: first, "nowhere in either his published or unpublished works of the 1790s does he issue any sort of

---

[30] For related discussion see Louden (2000, pp. 82–104; 2011, pp. 128–35, 150–63).

[31] See Girtanner (1796). At the beginning of his unpaginated preface, Girtanner writes: "The great Königsberg philosopher, in three essays on the human races that have been placed in various journals, has expressed some highly penetrating ideas .... I believe I am providing a service to all investigators of nature when I here present the system of the great thinker in so far as it is contained in these essays, bring his ideas together, and present his theory for the most part in his own words" (Girtanner 1796, unpaginated; cf. Mikkelsen 2013, pp. 210–11).

explicit *mea culpa* and acknowledge to readers that he has changed his mind about race" (Louden 2011, p. 134; see also Wood 2008, p. 10). Wouldn't an author who decided to change his mind about such a momentous issue also choose to acknowledge that he had done so in print? Second, when we take the time to examine what Girtanner "has presented so beautifully in explanation and further development" of Kant's views about race in his own 422-page book, we unfortunately find multiple descriptions and endorsements of Kant's hierarchical account of the race. For instance, in his *Ueber das Kantische Prinzip für die Naturgeschichte*, Girtanner writes: "in nearly four hundred years, none of them [viz., the Gypsies] have become farmers or manual laborers .... Of the many thousands of negroes that one encounters in England and America, none pursues a business [*Geschäft*] that one could actually call work" (Girtanner 1796, p. 157; cf. ÜGTP 8: 174). Earlier in the book we are informed that "the weather-beaten skin of Negroes is so thick ... that, like oxhide, it could serve as soles of shoes," and that their "sweat is very offensive [*sehr übelriechend*]" (Girtanner 1796, pp. 109–10, 109; cf. BBMR 8: 103). And later we learn that "cultivated Europeans, who emigrate from Europe in order to cultivate the western region of North America ... become exactly as lazy and inactive, even as crude [*roh*], as the native savages [*Wilden*]" (Girtanner 1796, p. 216; cf. V-Anth/Mensch 25: 1187).[32]

But one complication in this ongoing debate hinges on the fact that in his later writings Kant does speak forcefully and clearly against European colonialist practices in Africa, Asia, and the Americas. For instance, in his discussion of abuses of the right to visit other countries in *Toward Perpetual Peace*, he writes:

the *inhospitable* behavior of civilized, especially commercial, states in our part of the world, the injustice they show in *visiting* foreign lands and peoples (which with them is tantamount to *conquering* them) goes to horrifying lengths. When America, the negro countries, the Spice Islands, the Cape, and so forth were discovered, they were, to them, countries belonging to no one, since they counted the inhabitants as nothing. In the East Indies (Hindustan), they brought in foreign soldiers under the pretext of merely proposing to set up trading posts, but with them oppression of the inhabitants, incitement of the various Indian states to widespread wars, famine, rebellion, treachery, and the whole litany of troubles that oppress the human race .... The worst of this (or, considered from the standpoint of a moral judge, the best) is that these commercial states do not even profit from this violence; that

---

[32] As we saw earlier, Girtanner emphasizes in his preface that his goal is to "present his [viz., Kant's] theory for the most part in his own words," and to achieve this goal it would seem that he would necessarily have to include Kant's hierarchical account of race. Kleingeld's claim that Girtanner's discussion of race focuses "strictly on race as a physiological concept ... omitting any 'moral characterization'" (Kleingeld 2012, p. 115) is, I think, incorrect.

> all these trading companies are on the verge of collapse; that the Sugar
> Islands, that place of the cruelest and most calculated slavery, yield no true
> profit but serve only a mediate and indeed not very laudable purpose. (ZeF 8:
> 358–9)

Similarly, in his discussion of the acquisition of property in the *Metaphysics of Morals*, Kant states:

> it can still be asked whether … we should not be authorized to found
> colonies, by force if need be, in order to establish a civil union with them
> and bring these human beings (savages) into a rightful condition (as with the
> American Indians, the Hottentots, and the inhabitants of New Holland); or
> (which is not much better) to found colonies by fraudulent purchase of their
> land, and so become owners of their land, making use of our superiority
> without regard for their first possession. Should we not be authorized to do
> this, especially since nature itself (which abhors a vacuum) seems to
> demand it, and great expanses of land in other parts of the world, which
> are now splendidly populated, would have otherwise remained uninhabited
> by civilized people or, indeed, would have to remain forever uninhabited, so
> that the end of creation would have been frustrated? But it is easy to see
> through this veil of injustice (Jesuitism), which would sanction any means
> to good ends; this manner of acquiring land is therefore reprehensible
> [*verwerflich*]. (MS 6: 266; cf. 353)[33]

Kant speaks unambiguously here: he is a strong critic of colonialism. But once we acknowledge this fact, a new problem arises. Given that racism and colonialism "have often appeared together … [and] have also been conceptually linked in various ways" (McCarthy 2009, p. 1), how can an author criticize colonialism while embracing racism? Don't racism and colonialism "clearly go hand in hand" (Kleingeld 2014, p. 47)? For those who hold that Kant eventually abandoned his racism, there is no dilemma here. But in my view, it remains as one of several unresolved tensions in Kant's outlook. Yes, Kant did reject colonialism. But he was not able to overcome his belief that non-whites, non-Western Europeans, and women were all inferior to white European heterosexual men.

Much ink has understandably been spilt on these topics in recent years, and – particularly given the recent and ongoing murders of people of color in the US and across the globe by systematically racist police forces – it seems safe to wager that we will hear yet more about them in the future. But there still remains the question of how to responsibly and accurately convey information regarding anthropological difference. How can and should "the most valuable part of the

---

[33] For further discussion, see Flikschuh and Ypi (2014), Williams (2014), and Elden and Mendieta (2011).

anthropological heritage: the critical awareness of our shared humanity" (Ellingson 2001, p. 388) be conveyed? What perspective will best enable anthropologists to "dispense with racial, ideological, and imperialist stereo-types" in order to engage in "the common enterprise of promoting common humanity" (Said 1979, p. 328)? Knowledge of national character, as Kant notes in *Pillau*, "is always a necessary prerequisite [*immer eine nothwendige Bedingung*] of *Weltkenntnis*" (V-Anth/Pillau 25: 831), and the same also holds for gender and race. Knowledge of these matters is necessary for the pragmatic mission of Kantian anthropology, which strengthens one's ability "to use other human beings skillfully for one's purposes" (Anth 7: 322).[34] But how can anthropologists discuss these topics without "turning distinction into discrim-ination and difference into deficiency" (Zöller 2011, p. 138)? Much as we might like to retreat to an easy position of "absolute incommensurability, and a consequent plurality of all cultures" (Pagden 1993, p. 183, cf. 186), this is not a viable option if we really wish to understand others or ourselves. What is needed is an account of otherness that makes sense of others' beliefs and lives, but one that also recognizes that they are sufficiently like us to make compari-sons possible. The track record of anthropology (Kantian and otherwise) on this issue is poor. A good starting point would be to take to heart Kant's observations that all human beings "are from one family" (Refl 1499, 15: 782) and that what is needed is a "*broadened* way of thinking" that enables us "to think from the standpoint of everyone else" (KU 5: 294). Kantian philosophy, in other words, would appear to possess the necessary resources to deal with this crucial issue. But Kant himself did not make sufficient use of them. He remained unable to find a balance between his ethical universalism and the diversity of world cultures.[35]

---

[34] Again, insofar as the existence of national character, gender, and race is the result of "the play of nature" rather than free human action, they are not properly counted as "pragmatic *Weltkenntnis*, but only as theoretical *Weltkenntnis*" (Anth 7: 120). But as discussed earlier in Section 2, pragmatic anthropology is also a doctrine of prudence that teaches us "how we can use human beings to our end" (V-Anth/Busolt 25: 1436) and "direct others according to our purposes" (V-Anth/Mensch 25: 855). In this latter sense, accurate and objective knowledge of national character, race, and gender all fall under the purview of pragmatic knowledge of the world.

[35] Schleiermacher's objections to Kant's *Anthropology* are by no means limited to the two issues discussed here. Frierson, for instance, holds that Schleiermacher's "most philosophically import-ant objection" (Frierson 2003, p. 1) against it is the claim that anthropology conflicts with transcendental freedom. In order to study human beings empirically and anthropologically, Schleiermacher argues, one needs to assume that "all free choice in human beings is nature" (Kant 1980, p. 340) – viz., causally determined. But according to Kant's theory of freedom, "all nature in human beings is free choice" (Kant 1980, p. 340) - viz., our individual nature is itself the result of free choice. Schleiermacher himself "solves" this dilemma simply by opting for a version of determinism over free will, which I do not regard as an advance over Kant's position. For a detailed reply to Schleiermacher on this point, see Frierson (2003). For a reply to both

4.2 Pure and Impure

Related to the charge that Kantian anthropology is merely a popular and unsystematic project aiming at *Weltkenntnis* rather than a scholarly, academic pursuit is the claim that it is not properly philosophical but simply empirical. Brandt has voiced this objection repeatedly in his writings. "Empirical, pragmatic anthropology is not a part of philosophy in the strict sense" (Brandt 1994, p. 17). "Pragmatic anthropology ... neither belongs to philosophy in the strict sense, nor is it articulated as a system based upon an idea of reason. It is an empirical discipline" (Brandt 2003, p. 85; cf. Brandt and Stark 1997, 25: xii n., xiii). Similarly, Zammito, in his defense of Herder's anthropology over Kant's, argues that "Kant created the 'critical philosophy' at the cost of forsaking the 'science' of anthropology. He sought to *relegate* it – not *promote* it – to the 'pragmatic'" (Zammito 2002, p. 348). "The critical Kant showed no interest in displacing philosophy with anthropology, but insisted upon its proper subordination to philosophy" (Zammito 2002, p. 182; cf. 3, 299).

I argued earlier (see Sections 2 and 3) that Kant's anthropology (some of his own remarks to the contrary) is not merely empirical. It includes normative, teleological, and conceptual dimensions that take it far beyond the confines of a mere *Beobachtungslehre*. The point bears repeating here, for one straightforward reply to those who equate Kant's philosophy with the nonempirical and who then criticize Kantian anthropology for being merely empirical and hence unphilosophical is simply to point out that Kantian anthropology is in fact not merely empirical. But there is also the further issue of whether Kant's philosophy blocks out the empirical in the draconian manner claimed by Brandt and Zammito. Granted, Kant does occasionally talk this way. For instance, toward the end of the first *Critique* he states that "metaphysics ... alone [*allein*] properly constitutes what we can call philosophy, in the genuine sense of the term [*im echten Verstande*]" (KRV A 850/B 878). However, only a few pages earlier he also writes: "All philosophy ... is either knowledge from pure reason, or rational cognition from empirical principles. The former is called pure, the latter empirical philosophy" (KrV A 840/B 868; cf. A 848/B 876). Similarly, in the preface to the *Groundwork* Kant notes: "One can call all philosophy, insofar as it is based on grounds of experience, *empirical*, but that which puts forth its doctrines solely from principles *a priori*, *pure* philosophy.... Physics will thus have its empirical but also a rational part; and ethics likewise" (GMS 4: 388; cf. PhilEnz 29: 7). And in his discussion of philosophy in *The Conflict of the Faculties* he notes that

---

Schleiermacher and Frierson on the issue of freedom and anthropology, see Louden (2018 c). For further discussion of Schleiermacher, see Louden (2013).

the philosophy faculty consists of two departments: a department of *historical knowledge* (to which history, geography, philology, and the humanities all belong, along with all the empirical knowledge contained in the natural sciences), and a department of pure rational knowledge (pure mathematics and pure philosophy, metaphysics of nature and morals). (SF 7: 28)

So Kant's considered view, as well as the institutional reality of the time, was that philosophy consists of both a pure and an empirical part. And in fact a great deal of his own work – both before and after the "critical turn" of 1770 – has extensive empirical content. If we are to exclude anthropology from Kant's philosophy on the ground that it is merely empirical and insufficiently metaphysical, then a huge swath of his other writings will have to be tossed out with it – the lectures on geography and many of his publications on natural science, the lectures and essays on pedagogy, his essays on the philosophy of history, his numerous popular essays, and still more. Kant's philosophy is by no means limited to the a priori, and those who are obsessed with keeping philosophy pure have done him a great disservice in claiming otherwise.

I am not here attempting "a reenvisioning of the entire Kantian system as precisely an anthropology" (Zammito 2002, p. 349), nor am I undertaking "a substantial elevation of the status of anthropology in Kant's system"[36] (Zammito 2002, p. 351). Rather, I am merely trying to articulate Kant's position concerning anthropology's actual role within his own philosophy, a project that I pursue more explicitly in the next section. And in pursuing this goal I do intend to show that Kant's anthropological interest is much more than "a sideline to his main work in critical philosophy" or "a mere diversion from it" (Zöller 2011, p. 136).

4.3 "The Eye of True Philosophy"

The final criticism of Kantian anthropology to which I wish to reply comes from those who, while they do not object to including it as a legitimate component of Kant's philosophy, judge it to be inferior and unimportant in comparison with the transcendental Kant of the three *Critiques*.[37] As one recent commentator remarks, Kant's anthropological and popular writings are

shallow and unoriginal. It is hard to imagine that a Kant who had written even the best of his popular writings "What is Enlightenment?," say, or the

---

[36] Zammito singles out Wood's essay, "Unsociable Sociability: The Anthropological Basis of Kantian Ethics," as the chief culprit here. But despite the essay's provocative title, Wood is not challenging Kant's claim that "all moral philosophy must rest entirely on its pure part" (GMS 4: 389; cf. Wood 1994, p. 326). As he notes: "My defense of the thesis that Kantian ethics is based on anthropology should *not* be interpreted as a denial of Kant's fundamental notion of an a priori metaphysics of morals" (Wood 1994, p. 348 n.2).

[37] In this section I borrow from the last part of Louden (2020).

"Theory and Practice" essay – would be remembered today as more than a minor scribbler of the 18th century, and that a Kant who had written just the *Anthropology* and the *Physical Geography* would be remembered at all …. It is a mistake to suggest that these pieces should be given the same serious attention that the … three *Critiques* deserve. (Fleischacker 2018, n.p.)[38]

In what follows I shall respond to the popular charge that Kantian anthropology is shallow and unoriginal. Again, in my view Kant the anthropologist is an important and original thinker whose insights add value to the significance of his overall philosophical project. And while I argued earlier (see Section 3) against his reductionist claim that one could reckon all of philosophy "as anthropology" (Log 9: 25), I do think that, for humans, true philosophy in Kant's sense requires anthropology and that Kantian anthropology is ultimately what grounds philosophy and gives it dignity.

In the same *Reflexion* where Kant raises the alluring prospect of an *anthropologia transcendentalis*, he also criticizes an increasingly familiar kind of scholar who lacks humanity and "trusts his own powers too much" (Refl 903, 15: 395). Max Weber would later famously describe such a person as a "specialist without spirit" (Weber 1958, p. 182), but Kant says: "I call such a person a Cyclops" (Refl 903, 15: 395). This one-eyed giant (Kant is alluding to a famous passage in Homer's *Odyssey*),[39] he adds, "needs another eye, so that he can consider his object from the point of view of other human beings" (Refl 903, 15: 395). This necessary second eye, which is precisely what specialists without spirit lack, is "what grounds the humanity of the sciences; that is, gives them the affability of judgment through which one submits to the judgment of others" (Refl 903, 15: 395).

The scholarly Cyclops thus needs to acquire some humanity by cultivating a broadened way of thinking, one that will enable him to "think into the place of the other" (Anth 7: 200). In the *Anthropology*, Kant also notes that despite the "*gigantic* erudition" of the Cyclops, he "lacks one eye, the eye of true philosophy [*das (Auge) der wahren Philosophie*], by means of which human reason appropriately uses this mass of historical knowledge, the load of a hundred camels" (Anth 7: 227). Similarly, in criticizing "*cyclopic* learnedness" in the lectures on logic recorded by Jäsche, he remarks that this narrow-minded scholarship

---

[38] Fleischacker's comments here are directed against Louden (2017). Elsewhere in his review he writes: "If, when Louden says that these works are underappreciated, he means simply that they are underappreciated *as a key to what Kant believed*, he may well be right. But if he means that these works, especially the writings on anthropology, are underappreciated *in quality*, then I wonder if he can possibly be serious" (Fleischacker 2018, n.p.). I am serious.

[39] In the *Odyssey*, Odysseus escapes from the Cyclops by seizing a "fire-point-hardened timber" and twirling it in the giant's eye socket until "the roots of his eye crackle" (Homer 1965, p. 147).

lacks one eye, the eye of philosophy [*das Auge der Philosophie*], and a Cyclops among mathematicians, historians, natural historians, philologists, and linguists is a scholar who is great in all these matters, but who for all that holds philosophy to be dispensable. (Log 9: 45)

The underlying message in these passages is that one-eyed scholars (whose ranks within philosophy and other areas of academia have unfortunately swelled since Kant's day) need to acquire a broader, more humanistic way of thinking, one that Kant elsewhere calls "philosophy in the *cosmopolitan* sense (*in sensu cosmopolitico*)" (V-Met-L2/Pölitz 28: 532), "philosophy according to the world concept [*Philosophie nach dem Weltbegriffe*] (*in sensu cosmico*)" (Log 9: 24; cf. 23), and "the science of the ultimate ends of human reason" (V-Met-L2/Pölitz 28: 532; cf. Log 9: 23). This "high concept" of philosophy in the cosmopolitan sense, he adds, "gives philosophy dignity; i.e., an absolute worth [*Würde, d i. einen absoluten Werth*]" (Log 9: 23), and it also "gives a worth to all other sciences" (V-Met-L2/Pölitz 28: 532; cf. Log 9: 24). Similarly, in the first *Critique* he writes: "Until now ... the concept of philosophy has been only a *scholastic concept* [*nur ein Schulbegriff*] .... But there is also a *world concept* [*einen Weltbegriff*] (*conceptus cosmicus*) that has always grounded [*jederzeit zum Grude gelegen hat*] this term" (KrV A 838/B 866).

But philosophy in this cosmopolitan and humanistic sense – philosophy according to the world concept – is made possible only by anthropology. For it rests on a broad-based and empirically informed grasp of human nature. Anthropology from a Kantian point of view is ultimately what grounds philosophy and gives it dignity and inner worth, but not because all of philosophy's questions are resolved by answering the single question, "*Was ist der Mensch?*". As I argued in Section 3, this claim is false, for philosophy is bigger than the merely human. Rather, anthropology grounds philosophy because philosophy, *for humans*, requires reflection on what it means to be a human being and on human beings' place in the universe, and because Kantian anthropology is precisely the discipline that provides us with this knowledge. Philosophy according to the world concept involves broad empirical knowledge of human beings – knowledge of their nature and the world they live in. Philosophy in the cosmopolitan sense requires an empirical and humanistic eye that gives its possessors a broadened way of thinking, one that includes knowledge of human nature and of humanity's essential ends. Without this anthropological grounding, philosophy devolves into a mere intellectual parlor game or what Kant calls a *Schulbegriff* – a style of philosophy, as we have seen, from which one cannot "obtain any Enlightenment for common life" (V-Anth/Mensch 25: 853). At least for humans, philosophy ultimately gets its importance from reflection on the question "What does it mean to be a human being?". This is

Kant's considered position, and his stance is a prime example in support of the claim that "the greatest philosophy is inspired by and inspires passionate engagement with the problems important to human life" (Van Norden 2017, p. 158). So, yes, Kantian anthropology is a "popular philosophy or philosophy for living" (Brandt 1994, p. 17), but it is also much more than this. It is ultimately what grounds Kant's philosophy. And, yes, "the contrast between 'philosophy, according to the academic concept' and 'philosophy, according to the world concept'" stands "at the core of Kant's whole sense of his *pedagogical* mission" (Zammito 2002, p. 286 – my emphasis), but it also stands at the core of his *philosophical* mission. Anthropology is the eye of true philosophy, and philosophy without anthropology – at least for humans – lacks dignity and inner worth.

4.4 Kant's Legacy to Philosophical Anthropology

In continental philosophy, the term "philosophical anthropology" traditionally denotes a specific school or tradition within twentieth-century German philosophy, associated most prominently with the works of Max Scheler, Helmuth Plessner, and Arnold Gehlen (see Scheler 2009; Plessner 2019; Gehlen 1988). Philosophical anthropology in this more specific sense is often said to have begun in 1928, when Scheler's *Die Stellung des Menschen im Kosmos* (The Human Place in the Cosmos) and Plessner's *Die Stufen des Organischen und der Mensch* (The Levels of Organic Life and the Human Being) were both first published. In its desire to arrive at *"one uniform idea of the human being"* (Scheler 2009, p. 5), this movement clearly owes a strong debt to Kantian anthropology, as do earlier efforts in philosophical anthropology in the nineteenth century (e.g., Feuerbach and Nietzsche) as well as more recent ones (see, e.g., Schacht 1990).

So we know that philosophical anthropology has a past; a past that owes much to Kant. But does it have a future? It is no secret that Kant's legacy to philosophical anthropology is currently being challenged on multiple fronts. Human beings' future on earth is itself now in jeopardy, and critics of the Anthropocene increase daily. While it is not yet clear whether the efforts of artificial intelligence and posthumanism theorists will be able to offer a viable nonhuman alternative once *Homo sapiens* ceases to exist, many of them are already convinced that the capacities for self-consciousness and philosophical reflection are not unique to humans. And don't forget the extraterrestrials – even though Kant's cautionary note that "we have no knowledge of *non-terrestrial* rational beings" (Anth 7: 321) continues to hold, despite the continued, massive, and costly efforts of numerous governmental and private agencies to prove otherwise. Still, even after humans do eventually disappear, our posthuman descendants (and/or our extraterrestrial neighbors) may well still ask: "What is (or was) the human being?". The question of what it means to be a human being and to live a human life will remain a compelling question, even when humans are no longer around to ask it.[40]

---

[40] I would like to thank Howard Williams, Allen Wood, Andrew Jones, Jodie Heap, Michael Kryluk, and the anonymous reviewers chosen by Cambridge University Press for helpful comments and suggestions on an earlier draft of this manuscript.

Sources

Baumgarten, Alexander (2013). *Metaphysics: A Critical Translation with Kant's Elucidations, Selected Notes, and Related Materials*, trans. and ed. Courtney D. Fugate and John Hymers. London: Bloomsbury.

Brandt, Reinhard (1994). "Ausgewählte Probleme der kantischen Anthropologie," in *Der ganze Mensch: Anthropologie und Literatur im 18. Jahrhundert*, ed. Hans-Jürgen Schings. Stuttgart: J. B. Metzler, 14–32.

(1999). *Kritischer Kommentar zu Kants Anthropologie in pragmatischer Hinsicht (1798)*. Hamburg: Meiner.

(2003). "The Guiding Idea of Kant's Anthropology and the Vocation of the Human Being," in *Essays on Kant's Anthropology*, ed. Brian Jacobs and Patrick Kain. Cambridge: Cambridge University Press, 85–104.

(2007). *Die Bestimmung des Menschen bei Kant*. Hamburg: Meiner.

Brandt, Reinhard and Werner Stark (1997). "Einleitung," in *Vorlesungen über Anthropologie*, ed. Berlin-Brandenburg Academy of Sciences. Berlin: De Gruyter, vii–cli (= vol. 25 of *Kant's gesammelte Schriften*).

Brinton, Crane, ed. (1956). *The Portable Age of Reason Reader*. New York: Viking Press.

Buber, Martin (1965). *Between Man and Man*. New York: Macmillan.

Cassirer, Ernst (1944). *An Essay on Man: An Introduction to a Philosophy of Human Culture*. Garden City, NY: Doubleday & Company, Inc.

Cicero (1971). *Tusculan Disputations*, trans. J. E. King. Loeb Classical Library. Cambridge, MA: Harvard University Press.

Cohen, Alix (2009). *Kant and the Human Sciences: Biology, Anthropology and History*. London: Palgrave Macmillan.

Elden, Stuart and Eduardo Mendieta, eds. (2011). *Reading Kant's Geography*. Albany, NY: State University of New York Press.

Ellingson, Ter (2001). *The Myth of the Noble Savage*. Berkeley, CA: University of California Press.

Fellini, Julian (2008). "Skizze einer transzendental Anthropologie bei Kant," in *Recht und Frieden ind der Philosophie Kants: Akten des X. Internationalen Kant-Kongresses*, ed. Valério Rohden . Berlin: De Gruyter, 23–32.

Firla, Monika (1981). *Untersuchungen zum Verhältnis von Anthropologie und Moralphilosophie*. Frankfurt: Peter Lang.

Fleischacker, Samuel (2018). Review of Elizabeth Robinson and Chris W. Suprenant (eds.), *Kant and the Scottish Enlightenment*. New York: Routledge, 2017. *Notre Dame Philosophical Reviews* 2018.02.14, URL = https://ndpr.nd.edu/news/kant-and-the-scottish-enlightenment.

Flikschuh, Katrin and Lea Ypi, eds. (2014). *Kant and Colonialism*. Oxford: Oxford University Press.

Foucault, Michel (1973). *The Order of Things*, trans. Alan Sheridan. New York: Vintage Books.

(2008). *Introduction to Kant's Anthropology*, ed. and trans. Robert Nigro and Kate Briggs.Los Angeles: Semiotext(e).

Frierson, Patrick R. (2003). *Freedom and Anthropology in Kant's Moral Philosophy*. Cambridge: Cambridge University Press.

(2013). *What Is the Human Being?* London: Routledge.

Geertz, Clifford (2000). *Available Light: Anthropological Reflections on Philosophical Topics*. Princeton, NJ: Princeton University Press.

Gehlen, Arnold (1988). *Man, His Nature and Place in the World*, trans. Clare McMillan and Karl Pillemer. New York: Columbia University Press.

Girtanner, Christoph (1796). *Ueber das Kantische Prinzip für die Naturgeschichte. Ein Versuch, diese Wissenschaft philosophisch zu behandeln*. Göttingen: Vandenhoeck und Ruprecht.

Hampshire, Stuart (1960). *Thought and Action*. New York: Viking Press.

Heidegger, Martin (1997). *Kant and the Problem of Metaphysics*, 5th ed., enlarged, trans. Richard Taft. Bloomington, IN: Indiana University Press.

Hinske, Norbert (1966). "Kants Idee der Anthropologie," in *Die Frage nach dem Menschen: Aufriss einer philosophischen Anthropologie. Festschrift für Max Müller zum 60. Geburtstag*, ed. Heinrich Rombach. Freiburg and Munich: Karl Alber, 410–27.

Homer (1965). *The Odyssey*, trans. Richmond Lattimore. New York: Harper & Row.

Hume, David (1975). *Enquiries Concerning Human Nature and Concerning the Principles of Morals*, ed. L. A. Selby-Bigge, 3rd ed. Oxford: Clarendon Press.

(1978). *A Treatise of Human Nature*, ed. L. A. Selby-Bigge, 2nd ed. Oxford: Clarendon Press.

Hutcheson, Francis (1994). *Philosophical Writings*, ed. R. S. Downie. London: Dent.

Jachmann, Reinhold Bernhard (1804). *Immanuel Kant geschildert in Briefen an einen Freund*. Königsberg: Friedrich Nicolovius.

Kain, Patrick (2003.) "Prudential Reason in Kant's Anthropology," in *Essays on Kant's Anthropology*, ed. Brian Jacobs and Patrick Kain. Cambridge: Cambridge University Press, 230–65.

Kant, Immanuel (1980). *Anthropologie in pragmatischer Hinsicht*, ed. Karl Vorländer, with an introduction by Joachim Kopper and a supplementary appendix by Rudolf Malter. Hamburg: Felix Meiner.

Kaulbach, Friedrich (1966). "Weltorientierung, Weltkenntnis und pragmatische Vernunft bei Kant," in *Kritik und Metaphysik. Studien: Heinz Heimsoeth zum achtzigsten Geburtstag*, ed. Friedrich Kaulbach and Joachim Ritter. Berlin: Walter de Gruyter, 60–75.

Kleingeld, Pauline (2007). "Kant's Second Thoughts on Race," *The Philosophical Quarterly* 57: 573–92.

(2012). *Kant and Cosmopolitanism: The Philosophical Ideal of World Citizenship*. Cambridge: Cambridge University Press.

(2014). "Kant's Second Thoughts on Colonialism," in *Kant and Colonialism*, ed. Katrin Flikschuh and Lea Ypi. Oxford: Oxford University Press, 43–67.

Kowalewski, Arnold, ed. (1924). *Die philosophischen Hauptvorlesungen Immanuel Kants. Nach den neu aufgefundenen Kolleghfeten des Grafen Heinrich zu Dohna-Wundlacken*. Munich and Leipzig: Rösl & Cie.

Linden, Mareta (1976). *Untersuchungen zum Anthropologiebegriff des 18. Jahrhunderts*. Frankfurt am Main: Peter Lang.

Lorini, Gaultiero (2018). "The Rules for Knowing the Human Being: Baumgarten's Presence in Kant's Anthropology," in *Knowledge, Morals and Practice in Kant's Anthropology*, ed. Gualtiero Lorini and Robert B. Louden. London: Palgrave Macmillan, 63–80.

Louden, Robert B. (2000). *Kant's Impure Ethics: From Rational Beings to Human Beings*. New York: Oxford University Press.

(2011). *Kant's Human Being: Essays on His Theory of Human Nature*. New York: Oxford University Press.

(2013). "Schleiermacher, Friedrich," in the *International Encyclopedia of Ethics*, ed. Hugh LaFollette. Hoboken, NJ: Wiley-Blackwell, 8: 4728–38.

(2014 a). "The Last Frontier: The Importance of Kant's *Geography*," *Society and Space* 32: 450–66. (Reprinted in *Reading Kant's Lectures*, ed. Robert R. Clewis. Berlin: De Gruyter, 2015, 507–25.)

(2014 b). "Cosmopolitical Unity: The Final Destiny of the Human Species," in *Kant's Lectures on Anthropology: A Critical Guide*, ed. Alix Cohen. Cambridge: Cambridge University Press, 211–29.

(2014 c). "Kantian Anthropology: A Science Like No Other," *Estudos Kantianos* 2: 201–15.

(2017). "A Writer More Excellent Than Cicero: Hume's Influence on Kant's Anthropology," in *Kant and the Scottish Enlightenment*, ed. Elizabeth Robinson and Chris W. Suprenant. London: Routledge, 164–80.

(2018 a). "Kant's Anthropology: (Mostly) Empirical Not Transcendental," in *Der Zyklop in der Wissenschaft: Kant und die anthropolgia transcendentalis*, ed. Francesco Valerio Tommasi. Hamburg: Felix Meiner, 19–33.

(2018 b). "The Moral Dimensions of Kant's Anthropology," in *Knowledge, Morals and Practice in Kant's Anthropology*, ed. Gualtiero Lorini and Robert B. Louden. London: Palgrave Macmillan, 101–16.

(2018 c). "Freedom from an Anthropological Point of View," in *Natur und Freiheit: Akten des XII. Internationalen Kant-Kongresses*, ed. Violette L. Waibel, Margit Ruffing, and David Wagner. Berlin: De Gruyter, 457–72.

(2021 a). "Lectures on Anthropology," in *The Cambridge Kant Lexicon*, ed. Julian Wuerth. Cambridge: Cambridge University Press, 756–60.

(forthcoming a). "Anthropology," in *The Kantian Mind*, ed. Sorin Baiasu and Mark Timmons. London: Routledge.

(forthcoming b). "Philosophical Anthropology," in *The Encyclopedia of Philosophy of Religion*, ed. Stewart Goetz and Charles Taliaferro. Hoboken, NJ: John Wiley & Sons.

(forthcoming c). "'An Illusion of Affability That Inspires Love': Kant on the Value and Disvalue of Politeness," in *The Philosophy of (Im)Politeness*, ed. Chaoqun Xie. New York: Springer.

(2021 b). "Humans-Only Norms: An Unexpected Kantian Story," in *Kant on Morality, Humanity, and Legality: Practical Dimensions of Normativity*, ed. Ansgar Lyssy and Christopher Yeomans. London: Palgrave Macmillan, 131–47.

(2020). "Kant the Naturalist," *Journal of Transcendental Philosophy* 1: 3–17.

(forthcoming d). "Foucault's Kant," *The Journal of Value Inquiry*.

McCarthy, Thomas (2009). *Race, Empire, and the Idea of Human Development*. Cambridge: Cambridge University Press.

Mellin, Georg Samuel (1970). *Enzyklopädisches Wörterbuch der kritischen Philosophie*, 6 vols. Aalen: Scientia Verlag.

Mensch, Jennifer (2018). "From Anthropology to Rational Psychology in Kant's *Lectures on Metaphysics*," in *Kant's Lectures on Metaphysics*, ed. Courtney D. Fugate. Cambridge: Cambridge University Press, 194–213.

Mikkelsen, Jon M., trans. and ed. (2013). *Kant and the Concept of Race: Late Eighteenth-Century Writings*. Albany, NY: State University of New York Press.

Muthu, Sankar (2003). *Enlightenment Against Empire*. Princeton, NJ: Princeton University Press.

Niquet, Marcel (2001). "Transzendentale Anthropologie und die Begründung der praktischen Philosophie," in *Kant und die Berliner Aufklärung: Akten des IX. Kant Kongresses*, ed. Volker Gerhardt, Rolf-Peter Horstmann, and Ralph Schumacher. Berlin: De Gruyter, 405–15.

Nobbe, Frank (1995). *Kants Frage nach dem Menschen: Die Kritik der ästhetischen Urteilskraft als transzentale Anthropologie*. Frankfurt: Peter Lang.

Pagden, Anthony (1993). *European Encounters with the New World.* New Haven, CT: Yale University Press.

Peacocke, Christopher (2004). "Moral Rationalism," *Journal of Philosophy* 101: 499–526.

Plato (1997). *Complete Works,* ed. John Cooper. Indianapolis, IN: Hackett Publishing Company.

Plessner, Helmuth (2019). *Levels of Organic Life: An Introduction to Philosophical Anthropology,* trans. Millay Hyatt. New York: Fordham University Press.

Rensch, Thomas (1990). *Die Konstitution der Moralität: Transzendentale Anthropologie und praktische Philosophie.* Frankfurt: Suhrkamp.

Rink, Friedrich Theodor (1805). *Ansichten aus Immanuel Kant's Leben.* Königsberg: Göbbels und Unzer.

Rorty, Richard (1982). "Keeping Philosophy Pure: An Essay on Wittgenstein," in Richard Rorty, *Consequences of Pragmatism.* Minneapolis, MN: University of Minnesota Press, 19–36.

Rousseau, Jean-Jacques (1964). *The First and Second Discourses,* ed. Roger D. Masters. New York: St. Martin's Press.

Said, Edward W. (1979). *Orientalism.* New York: Vintage Books.

Sánchez Madrid, Nuria (2018). "Controlling Mental Disorder: Kant's Account of Mental Illness in the Anthropology Writings," in *Knowledge, Morals and Practice in Kant's Anthropology,* ed. Gualtiero Lorini and Robert B. Louden. London: Palgrave Macmillan, 147–62.

Schacht, Richard (1990). "Philosophical Anthropology: What, Why and How," *Philosophy and Phenomenological Research* 50 (Supplement): 155–76.

Scheler, Max (2009). *The Human Place in the Cosmos,* trans. Manfred S. Frings. Evanston, IL: Northwestern University Press.

Schiller, Friedrich (1955). *Gedichte.* Wiesbaden: Insel-Verlag.

Schmid, Carl Christian Erhard (1976). *Wörterbuch zum leichtern Gebrauch der kantischen Schriften.* Darmstadt: Wissenschaftliche Buchgesellschaft.

Schmidt, Claudia M. (2007). "Kant's Transcendental, Empirical, Pragmatic, and Moral Anthropology," *Kant-Studien* 98: 156–82.

Shell, Susan Meld (1996). *The Embodiment of Reason: Kant on Spirit, Generation, and Community.* Chicago: University of Chicago Press.

Simmermacher, Volker (1951). "Kant's Kritik der reinen Vernunft als Grundlegung einer *Anthropologia Transcendentalis.*" PhD dissertation, Heidelberg.

Stark, Werner (2003). "Historical Notes and Interpretive Questions about Kant's Lectures on Anthropology," in *Essays on Kant's Anthropology,* ed. Brian Jacobs and Patrick Kain. Cambridge: Cambridge University Press, 15–37.

Sturm, Thomas (2009). *Kant und die Wissenschaften vom Menschen.* Paderborn: Mentis.

Van de Pitte, Frederick P. (1971). *Kant as Philosophical Anthropologist.* The Hague: Martinus Nijhoff.

Van Norden, Bryan W. (2017). *Taking Back Philosophy: A Multicultural Manifesto.* New York: Columbia University Press.

Vorländer, Karl (2003). *Immanuel Kant: Der Mann und das Werk*, special ed. after the 3rd expanded ed. of 1992. Wiesbaden: Fourier.

Weber, Max (1958). *The Protestant Ethic and the Spirit of Capitalism*, trans. Talcott Parsons. New York: Charles Scribner's Sons.

Weiler, Gershohn (1980). "Kant's Question 'What Is Man?'", *Philosophy of the Social Sciences* 10: 1–23.

Williams, Howard (2014). "Colonialism in Kant's Political Philosophy," *Diametros* 39: 154–81.

Willich, A. F. M. (1798). *Elements of the Critical Philosophy.* London: Longman.

Wilson, Holly L. (2006). *Kant's Pragmatic Anthropology: Its Origin, Meaning, and Critical Significance.* Albany, NY: State University of New York Press.

(2018). "Elucidation of the Sources of Kant's Anthropology," in *Knowledge, Morals and Practice in Kant's Anthropology*, ed. Gualtiero Lorini and Robert B. Louden. London: Palgrave Macmillan, 11–28.

Wood, Allen W. (1994). "Unsociable Sociability: The Anthropological Basis of Kantian Ethics," *Philosophical Topics* 19: 325–51.

(2008). *Kantian Ethics.* Cambridge: Cambridge University Press.

(2012). "General Introduction," in Immanuel Kant, *Lectures on Anthropology*, ed. Allen W. Wood and Robert B. Louden. Cambridge: Cambridge University Press, 1–10.

Zammito, John H. (2002). *Kant, Herder, and the Birth of Anthropology.* Chicago: University of Chicago Press.

(2014). "What a Young Man Needs for His Venture into the World: The Function and Evolution of the 'Characteristics'," in *Kant's Lectures on Anthropology: A Critical Guide*, ed. Alix Cohen. Cambridge: Cambridge University Press, 230–48.

Zöller, Günter (2011). "Kant's Political Anthropology," *Kant Yearbook* 3: 131–61.

In memory of my brother, David Bruce Louden (1954–2020)

Cambridge Elements ☰

The Philosophy of Immanuel Kant

Desmond Hogan
Princeton University
Desmond Hogan joined the philosophy department at Princeton in 2004. His interests include Kant, Leibniz and German rationalism, early modern philosophy, and questions about causation and freedom. Recent work includes "Kant on Foreknowledge of Contingent Truths," *Res Philosophica* 91 (1) (2014); "Kant's Theory of Divine and Secondary Causation," in Brandon Look (ed.) *Leibniz and Kant*, Oxford University Press (forthcoming); "Kant and the Character of Mathematical Inference," in Carl Posy and Ofra Rechter (eds.) *Kant's Philosophy of Mathematics Vol. I*, Cambridge University Press (forthcoming).

Howard Williams
University of Cardiff
Howard Williams was appointed Honorary Distinguished Professor at the Department of Politics and International Relations, University of Cardiff in 2014. He is also Emeritus Professor in Political Theory at the Department of International Politics, Aberystwyth University, a member of the Coleg Cymraeg Cenedlaethol (Welsh-language national college), and a Fellow of the Learned Society of Wales. He is the author of *Marx* (1980); *Kant's Political Philosophy* (1983); *Concepts of Ideology* (1988); *International Relations in Political Theory* (1992); *Hegel, Heraclitus and Marx's Dialectic*; *International Relations and the Limits of Political Theory* (1996); *Kant's Critique of Hobbes: Sovereignty and Cosmopolitanism* (2003), and *Kant and the End of War* (2012) and is currently editor of the journal *Kantian Review*. He is writing a book on the Kantian Legacy in Political Philosophy for a new series edited by Paul Guyer.

Allen Wood
Indiana University
Allen Wood is Ward W. and Pricilla B. Woods Professor at Stanford University. He was a John S. Guggenheim Fellow at the Free University in Berlin, a national Endowment for the Humanities Fellow at the University of Bonn, and Isaiah Berlin Visiting Professor at the University of Oxford. He is on the editorial board of eight philosophy journals, five book series, and the *Stanford Encyclopedia of Philosophy*. Along with Paul Guyer, Professor Wood is co-editor of the *Cambridge Edition of the Works of Immanuel Kant* and translator of the *Critique of Pure Reason*. He is the author or editor of a number of other works, mainly on Kant, Hegel, and Karl Marx. His most recent book, *Fichte's Ethical Thought*, was published by Oxford University Press in 2016. Wood is a member of the American Academy of Arts and Sciences.

About the Series
This Cambridge Elements series provides an extensive overview of Kant's philosophy and its impact upon philosophy and philosophers. Distinguished Kant specialists will provide an up-to-date summary of the results of current research in their fields and give their own take on what they believe are the most significant debates influencing research, drawing original conclusions.

Cambridge Elements $^{\equiv}$

The Philosophy of Immanuel Kant

Elements in the Series

A full series listing is available at: www.cambridge.org/EPIK

Printed in the United States
by Baker & Taylor Publisher Services